PRAISE FOR BELONGING AT WORK

❝ *Belonging at Work* is long overdue. Rhodes Perry's work is a testament to the power of living with authenticity at all hours of the day, at home and at work. Wherever you are in your journey of living an authentic, purposeful life, this book is a powerful tool that should be required reading in all workplaces that value diversity and full inclusion. ❞

— James R. Nowlin, CEO of EGP Ventures, Keynote Speaker,
and Best-Selling Author of The Purposeful Millionaire

❝ Our work environments are changing in dynamic ways. Rhodes Perry's new book *Belonging at Work*, is a keen guide to engaging in that change through positivity and action. Both powerful, and easy to navigate, Rhodes' guide to transforming company culture through inclusion, communication, and empowerment is a worthwhile and timely read. No matter where you are in your personal career journey, from employee to entrepreneur to leader, *Belonging at Work* is a valuable tool that will, undoubtedly, help move the needle in the direction of authenticity. ❞

— Hunter Sunrise, Founder & CEO, Hot Diggity!

❝ Rhodes Perry is an invaluable and important voice on our emerging understanding of what makes truly great workplace cultures: the ability for *all* of us to bring our full selves to work. He clearly lays out what gets in the way of this, particularly for those who are underrepresented, and historically undervalued, both from a personal lens of his LGBTQ experience, and on behalf of so many other lost and marginalized voices. Make no mistake, organizations and their bottom lines suffer from unexplored exclusionary practices. The book is full of practical examples of how we all have a role to play in redirecting the dynamics of exclusion, so that all in the workplace can thrive. A must read! ❞

— Jennifer Brown, President & CEO, Jennifer Brown Consulting, and
Best-Selling Author, Inclusion: Diversity, the New Workplace & the Will to Change

“ Transgender people have been chronically underemployed and under-valued in the social and corporate landscape for quite some time. However, it would be a mistake to read this book and think it only applies to transgender people or LGBTQ people. The reality is that the sense of belonging – the feeling of safety, community, and esteem – is something that we all crave in the workplace environment. Not only does a sense of belonging emancipate the employee, it also liberates companies to be true engines for innovation, growth, and sustainability. *Belonging at Work* is an instructive account of how organizations and companies can begin the journey of creating belonging in a thoughtful and strategic way. ”

– Joel Brown, Ed.D., Chief Visionary Officer, Pneumos, LLC

“ Conversations around diversity at work can be shallow. *Belonging at Work* is different. It provides a focused, practical, and holistic approach to truly creating an environment of inclusion and belonging. It provides smart, concise advice that any organization can implement to create a culture where everyone can thrive. ”

– Bernadette Smith, Founder & CEO, Equality Institute

“ *Belonging at Work* is a much needed balm in divisive times. The workplace is one of the few places where people from different backgrounds leave their curated lives and come together to share space and purpose. Rhodes Perry does a phenomenal job distilling complicated concepts of identity and walking the reader through the process of creating a workplace that works for them. The book is accessible for those new to the workplace inclusion field and an invaluable tool for those developing dynamic and cutting edge programs. ”

– Genesis Fischer, Esq., Founder and Principal Attorney,
Fisher Law Practice, P.C.

“ Creating safe and inclusive work environments is one of the greatest challenges for businesses and organizations today, and yet many leaders don't know where to start. *Belonging at Work* guides leaders through squaring their values at work with their organizational practices. After reading this book, you'll better understand *why* this work is critical to creating workplaces where individuals and teams can thrive and *how* to get started and make progress on your journey. 🔊

— *Martha Pellegrino, Founder & Chief Bravissima Officer, Brava Point LLC*

🔊 Rhodes Perry mixes personal story with practical and actionable strategies to make *Belonging at Work* a reality for everyone. From the consideration of the implicit culture being created when there is no intentional culture, to the definitions for diversity, equity, and inclusion, this book is a road map for the company of the future. 🔊

— *Judy Hissong, Founder and Chief Executive Officer, Nesso Strategies*

🔊 *Belonging at Work* is a must-read resource for team members in any business role. Rhodes Perry demonstrates the importance of becoming an inclusive leader. Readers will finish this book and come away with an evolved thought process and an actionable list. Whether you are a business person in a leadership role or someone who wants to understand the importance of being authentic at work, the learning is immense. Rhodes is a leader among leaders. His great outreach has affected many individuals. Bravo! 🔊

— *Andrew Cramer, CEO, Alternative Spaces Inc.,*
ROIGenius, ExtendATouch

🔊 Rhodes Perry has written a must-read primer for anyone interested in helping their organization become more inclusive. Do yourself and your organization a favor, and pick up a copy of *Belonging at Work* today! A brilliant piece of work! 🔊

— *Ryan J. Wayman, West Region Vice President,*
AXA Advisors, LLC

🔊 We are at a point in time where the data overwhelmingly points to the clear value that more diverse teams deliver. In order to realize this promise of diversity, we have to understand how to move beyond representation to creating cultures where everyone feels like they can deliver their best without fear or distraction. *Belonging at Work* lays the foundation for this journey. 🙶

— Stacy Parson, Partner, The Dignitas Agency

🙶 Rhodes Perry does an excellent job sharing *why* it's critical for business leaders to create workplace cultures of belonging. I especially liked the section of the book that focuses on the triple bottom line. Specifically, the importance of businesses leveraging their resources to invest in workplace giving and volunteerism. As the CEO of Bright Funds, a platform that helps businesses direct tens of millions of dollars in philanthropy, I know first-hand how these efforts help employees and other stakeholders feel a sense of meaning, purpose, and belonging at work all while creating more social good for the world. 🙶

— Ty Walrod, Chief Executive Officer,
Bright Funds and Co-Founder, OutServe

🙶 Rhodes is an amazing strategist who gives of himself unselfishly and is an advocate for all people. He takes his work to heart and overdelivers by creating an environment where we can all share our own stories. He is a change agent that is leading a culture of inclusiveness that will be instrumental in navigating humans to a happier and more sustainable existence. I fully encourage you to support and become engaged with his work. 🙶

— J. Robby Gregg, Jr., Engagement Lead, Cook Ross

🙶 Understanding and aligning around diversity, equity, and inclusion in a small business can be daunting, but *Belonging at Work* provides a clear, useful guide. Through my company's work with Rhodes we've seen a significant increase in the number of diverse candidates applying for positions and taken great strides toward becoming a more consciously inclusive and welcoming business. I'm delighted to have this book as a reference and refresher. 🙶

— Sarah Durham, CEO, Big Duck

❝ In the workplace we all want to be seen and heard and to have our ideas validated by our supervisors and peers alike. In this refreshingly new take on diversity and inclusion, Rhodes Perry's *Belonging at Work* gives companies and organizations no nonsense tools to ensure everyone feels safe, valued, and truly able to bring their authentic selves to their working environments, unencumbered by bias. ❞

– Cindi Creager, Co-Owner, CreagerCole Communications

❝ The concept of belonging may register as a soft skill and this is a common business mistake. Rhodes Perry does an excellent job of examining one of the hardest skills employers and employees have that directly impact recruitment and retention of talent and the organization's bottom line. Ideally, when we all belong, our organizations thrive. ❞

– Jessica Pettitt, Founder & CEO, Good Enough Now

❝ I've had the advantage of seeing Rhodes Perry create an inclusive and respectful workplace, guiding others to understand and value diversity. He is masterful in his approach and ability to engage people wherever they are in their own development and knowledge to help them implement change in the systems they lead. He has been able, in *Belonging at Work*, to convey his deep knowledge and experience in a very accessible and concrete manner. A must read! ❞

– Gladys Carrión, Esq., Former Commissioner,
New York City Administration for Children's Services

❝ Creating a workplace culture that welcomes all, embracing our diversity and lived experiences, is a challenge to many leaders. Rhodes provides practical and applicable strategies that will aid any leader in creating a workplace and culture where all feel a sense of belonging. Rhodes is an innovative thought leader and champion for diversity, equity, and inclusion. His insight and perspective are needed and so appreciated! ❞

– Scotty Scott, Senior Equity and Inclusion Specialist,
Multnomah County Office of Diversity and Equity

66 Having managed a large agency of 400 staff, I am acutely aware of how challenging it is – even for 'enlightened' organizations – to create environments that are both inclusive and celebratory of all people. Rhodes' book, *Belonging at Work*, is an invaluable resource to the field that sorely needs to do better. Organizations will be more likely to thrive when they provide the kind of organizational structure this book can help guide them to implement. 99

– Bill Bettencourt, Senior Fellow, The Center for the Study of Social Policy

66 Rhodes Perry's writing style clearly and gently guides the reader through understanding our basic human need for belonging and deftly outlines how to incorporate and commit to using diversity and inclusion practices and tools. Rhodes' professional expertise and lived experience steer the reader through the steps to achieve institutional change that results in true workplace equity, where people can thrive professionally in a place of belonging and success. 99

– Tatiana Elejalde, Office of Equity & Human Rights, City of Portland

66 *Belonging at Work* is an excellent, must-read resource for any worker, leader, or organization wanting to improve diversity, equity, and inclusion in their workplace. Rhodes brings a wealth of knowledge, experience, and skills to this book, whose well-researched concepts, useful glossary, and practical strategies are sure to help others cultivate more compassionate and productive workplace cultures where everyone feels they belong, are connected, and can grow without having to change themselves to fit in. 99

– Mary Celeste Kearney, Ph.D., Director of Gender Studies,
University of Notre Dame

66 As the father of a transgender man, I read *Belonging at Work* to gain insight to what my son experiences on a daily basis; I came away with tremendous respect for the bravery it takes to show up as your authentic self in the workplace. *Belonging at Work* provides a lens into how leaders must pivot to provide safe and nurturing environments for all employees. I found the book a great asset to recognize implicit

bias of leaders and the importance of utilizing a diversity lens in all workplace decisions. 🙶

🙸 Belonging. Connection. Authenticity. Each fosters wellness, reduces stress, and helps us create positive relationships, genuine communication, and constructive collaboration. They are central elements to human well-being, as well as to workplace performance and productivity. Rhodes Perry, in *Belonging at Work*, has written the essential book for the inclusive leader. True workplace inclusion is being able to fully participate, but full participation isn't just about policy. Rhodes skillfully guides readers through the necessary but all too often missing next step – covering the what, why, and the vital HOW to inform decisions through a diversity, equity and inclusion lens, and take action to effectively transform workplace culture. His book will equip you to act with intention and empathy, throughout your organization as well as within yourself. 🙶

🙸 Moving from the *why* to the *how* is one of the biggest challenges in any cultural change effort. In *Belonging at Work*, Rhodes Perry goes beyond providing the compelling case for truly inclusive workplace cultures and offers practical steps individuals and organizations can take. Having participated in an experiential exercise led by Rhodes, I can attest to the value of his approach to increasing empathy for those unlike ourselves and turning those personal insights into action that fosters meaningful change. 🙶

🙸 Leaders, prepare to be challenged and empowered: *Belonging at Work* is an essential guide to creating true inclusion. Read this if you want to create transformational change in your workplace. 🙶

66 Too often, organizations simply do not know how to operationalize values of inclusion and diversity. Rhodes offers tangible steps that can help catalyze action and movement toward an intentional work culture that lives its values. *Belonging at Work* is a book for anyone who has ever said, 'We really want to attract and retain a diverse team, but we cannot find candidates or when we do, they are not the right fit with our culture.' This book will help leaders understand what it takes to break down barriers that are preventing the shift that they want to make. 99

− Morey Riordan, Founding Director,
Transgender Strategy Center

66 *Belonging at Work* opens up the doors to understanding what diversity, equity, and inclusion look like in action by exploring Rhodes Perry's personal journey and realistic strategies. As a reader, you will instantly become connected with Rhodes' unique approach and experiences. As a leader of an organization, *Belonging at Work* is a must read for workplace success and development. 99

− Justin Nelson, Co-Founder and President,
National LGBTQ Chamber of Commerce

66 As more people become aware of the needs of an increasingly diverse workforce and are searching for help to achieve this, platitudes and lip service abound. *Belonging at Work* is the antidote to that. Rhodes Perry brings concrete advice and solid analysis from experienced professionals in corporate, government, and non-profit sectors alike. *Belonging at Work* is both a treasure trove of ideas and a road map for success. I'll be giving it to all my clients who are striving to be more effective and socially responsible leaders. 99

− Roey Thorpe, Advisor to Nonprofit Funders and Advocacy Organizations

66 Warm, insightful, strategic and long overdue for diversity and inclusions professionals, *Belonging at Work* helps home in on specific practices that create realistic results in the workplace. This book gives the platinum rules to follow for every

organization that pushes past the first step of opening the doors to diversity but actually doing the work to making people feel welcomed in the workplace. The book helps organizations make the rubber hit the road to success. It's a win-win for all when a worker can bring their full self to work. Rhodes Perry has done a phenomenal job in providing realistic and useful exercises to help improve anyone's diversity and inclusion practices. I strongly recommend this book be part of any diversity and inclusion professional's library. **"**

– Kylar W. Broadus, Esq., Global Human Rights Activist,
Lawyer, Business Law Professor

" Most people can remember a time when they felt like they didn't belong. In *Belonging at Work*, Rhodes Perry transforms this depressing reality into an empowering one. He shows how empathy and compassion around this universal need to belong are strengths we can all tap into while creating more inclusive workplaces. By centering the experiences of marginalized communities and breaking down concepts like "unconscious bias" and "stereotype threat," Rhodes supports readers at all experience levels in developing a diversity, equity and inclusion lens. Any manager who cares about the people they work with every day, sees differences within their team as a strength, and wants to make sure those differences are celebrated instead of hidden in their workplace will appreciate the concrete actions covered in this book. **"**

– Alison Delpercio, Director, All Children – All Families,
Human Rights Campaign Foundation

" My work with Rhodes Perry has been invaluable and his great work on the book, *Belonging at Work* has helped to improve my personal leadership skills… I walked away from the book with a better understanding for what it means to belong at work, why it matters for everyone my organization touches, and most importantly, I learned practical strategies to help cultivate a sense of belonging for the team I manage. Not only was it informative, but the exercises at the end of every chapter helped me consider how I could apply my learnings into my organization. I really connected with Rhodes' approach, and his guidance left me truly inspired. I highly recommend anyone who works on a team to pick up this book and begin the journey towards building a more inclusive workplace. **"**

– Kelli Houston, Director, Center for Diversity
and Health Equity, Seattle Children's Hospital

66 As an organizational leader, I have a responsibility to provide an environment where the people who come together to carry out our mission are able to be valued and supported in being their authentic selves. I find the insights that Rhodes has shared in *Belonging at Work* to be an invaluable tool to assist me in doing so. I heartily recommend the book. 99

— *Carl Siciliano, Founder and Executive Director, The Ali Forney Center*

66 The strategies featured in *Belonging at Work* were refined from Rhodes Perry's seasoned approach in supporting multiple organizations build more inclusive workplace cultures. The importance of belonging in non-profit organizations, especially where a majority of the organizational deliverables are accomplished through the effort of volunteers is critical. This book clearly provides a road map that leaders in volunteer organizations can utilize to attract and retain the talent and diversity today's non-profit organizations need to excel. 99

— *Danni/y Rosen, Co-Chair, GLSEN National Advisory Council and Board Member, Basic Rights Oregon*

66 *Belonging at Work* is essential reading for corporations and organizations willing to move beyond discussion of diversity, equity and inclusion (DEI) principles to their implementation in the workplace. The book provides a strategic plan for implementing inclusion practices by providing a concise, comprehensive analysis of workplace barriers that undermine such practices. *Belonging at Work* recognizes that there are steady challenges to effectuating lasting change in an organization's work culture and provides an inclusive and supportive plan for overcoming those challenges. Rhodes Perry's insight and intersectional analysis guides employers committed to eliminating workplace barriers that impair an employee's ability to belong at work. *Belonging at Work* is a roadmap for increasing workplace productivity by creating an environment where each employee belongs and thrives. Clearly, that is a winning combination that every employer should champion. 99

— *Linda Diaz, Esq., Director, LGBTQ Project, Lawyers for Children*

66 *Belonging at Work* is a must read for everyone who is committed to creating a workplace where individuals can live and breathe their best selves without judgment. It is a must read for all who journey to live authentically. Rhodes Perry provides the reader with intentional consciousness and practical exercises to create an environment of *Belonging at Work*. This book becomes a lasting resource beyond my organization's work with Rhodes. Brilliant! 55

– Dianna Kielian, Senior Vice President,
Mission / Theology & Ethics, PeaceHealth

66 Working alongside Rhodes Perry and his authentic, decisive, and humble leadership style made me a better leader, so it's no surprise that *Belonging at Work* took my leadership to the next level. Rhodes has created an accessible guide for us all, no matter where you are on your journey to creating or desiring to belong to an inclusive work place. *Belonging at Work* offers guidance, practical tools, and a supportive voice while you do this challenging and difficult work. This should be a must read for leaders in all industries interested in a thriving workforce. 55

– Sarah Mikhail, LMSW, Senior Director of Community Support.
The LGBT Community Center

66 Strategies for meaningful inclusion, connectivity and diversity are imperative in all workplaces – public sector, private sector and community-based organizations. *Belonging at Work* provides insightful and necessary guidance for managers and leaders in all sectors to develop and implement protocols to ensure that all employees are safe, valued and included at every level. 55

– Robyn Mazur, Director of Gender and Justice Initiatives,
Center for Court Innovation

BELONGING

AT WORK

BELONGING
AT WORK

Everyday Actions You Can Take to
Cultivate an Inclusive Organization

RHODES PERRY, MPA

ACADEMY
PRESS

For permission requests, write to the Author, addressed "Attention: Permissions Coordinator," at the address below:

RPC Academy Press
P.O. Box 6341
715 NW Hoyt Street
Portland, OR 97208

The opinions expressed by the Author are not necessarily those held by the PYP Academy Press.

Ordering information: Quantity sales and special discounts are available on quantity purchases by corporations, associations, and others. For details, contact the Author at the address above.

Edited by: Sarina Sandstrom
Cover design by: Nina Z.
Interior design by: Medlar Publishing Services Pvt Ltd, India

Printed in the United States of America.

ISBN – 978-1-7324419-0-3
Ebook – 978-1-7324419-8-9
Library of Congress Control Number: 2019935259

First edition, November 13, 2018

The information contained within this book is strictly for informational purposes. The material may include information, products, or services by third parties. As such, the Author and Publisher do not assume responsibility or liability for any third-party material or opinions. Readers are advised to do their own due diligence when it comes to making decisions.

The PYP Author's Academy and PYP Academy Press works with authors, and aspiring authors, who have a story to tell and a brand to build. Do you have a book idea you would like to be considered for publishing? Please visit PublishYourPurpose.com/academy for more information.

START HERE

Dear Reader,

Thank you for honoring me with your time and commitment to helping your people feel a sense of belonging at work. I am on a mission to empower leaders just like you – and those on their way to joining us – to cultivate workplace cultures of belonging.

Before diving into the content, this message offers important context as to how to leverage the book. The ideas in this book serve as a supplement rather than replacement to the guidance of working with a seasoned diversity, equity, and inclusion (DEI) professional.

While I am a DEI professional, the book's content is of an anecdotal and general nature that will inform your journey to cultivating workplace cultures of belonging. All efforts were made to verify the accuracy of the information featured in this book as of the date of publication.

You are encouraged to consult with your Chief Diversity Officer or other DEI professionals before adopting any of the suggestions in this book. This publication contains the opinions, ideas, and expertise of the author, as well as leading DEI thought leaders in the United States. The author and publisher specifically disclaim all responsibility for any liability, loss or risk, personal or otherwise, which is incurred as a consequence.

By reading this book you agree that neither my company, my publisher, nor myself are responsible for the success or failure of your business or life decisions relating to any information presented.

Now, together, let's learn more about what it means to belong at work, understand why it matters, and most importantly, learn how to cultivate this feeling for ourselves and our stakeholders.

Sincerely,

Rhodes Perry, MPA

DEDICATION

For those seeking a sense of purpose, meaning, and belonging in the workplace and beyond.

TABLE OF CONTENTS

FOREWORD

I met Rhodes Perry in 2016 and I was immediately impressed that he is the type of person who will be an outstanding leader in America's future. While we are not related by blood, he and I share the same surname and ideals when it comes to diversity, equity, and inclusion. He has devoted his career to creating fair treatment for all persons, which is an objective we all must share to achieve the ideals embedded in American democracy. I admire how he has used his education, experience, and courage to support leaders to include the voices of their stakeholders.

Rhodes has an impressive background of cross-sectional leadership with nearly two decades of experience working in government and nonprofit settings including the White House Office of Management and Budget, the New York City Office of LGBTQ Policy and Practice at the Administration for Children's Services, and leading the policy and advocacy efforts at PFLAG National.

He merged these experiences and established his own business, which specializes in helping leaders build inclusive organizations. He also shares his expertise through community volunteerism, serving as a Commissioner on the Portland Human Rights Commission and as a board member of the Portland Area Business Association where he works to expand economic opportunities for LGBTQ business owners.

Having the privilege of serving as a New York State Senator representing the Rochester-Monroe County area from 1975 to 1992, I am impressed by the fresh perspective Rhodes offers. He shares new ways of thinking about the workplace and the people involved, which diverges from the way the political process has traditionally interfaced between government and the private sector.

During my time as a New York State Senator, thousands of people came to my office seeking support for projects or policies they hoped the state would enact, reject, or repeal. Most of these requests came from leaders in the private sector seeking an economic advantage for themselves either by public funds supporting their private projects, or public funds being decreased to reduce their taxes.

From my experience, I sense that most people feel that in the world of business and politics if one person gains something of value it means that another person must lose something of equal value. Rhodes shares a new way of thinking about the role of business and politics; one where businesses can take care of their people, be good stewards of the planet, and profit.

In this book, Rhodes encourages leaders to examine their own workplace culture and move towards creating a harmonious atmosphere of belonging. By doing so, all stakeholders win the game. As the team's productivity increases, the organization has the opportunity to appeal to new markets, which ultimately increases profits and works to accomplishing the organization's mission. To create a belonging atmosphere requires everyone to look at the totality of other people and accept them as they are.

The principles and strategies Rhodes espouses can change many organizations for the better, whether in the public or the private sector. Certainly schools, federal, state, and local government agencies, and even religious organizations have much to gain in reading this book.

No matter where you work, what you do, where you are in the structure of your employment circumstances, Rhodes Perry's *Belonging at Work* will inspire you and make your job and workplace more valuable to everyone.

I must include one more aspect of my experience which I believe validates the importance of belonging. In 1976, New York Governor Hugh Carey appointed me to a national task force to improve the educational opportunities of migrant children as they traveled with their families who were picking crops from the south to the most northern states, even to New York. This task force eventually became a permanent entity, the Interstate Migrant Education Council (IMEC.) After I left the Senate I was the Executive Director of IMEC until I retired in 2010.

What I learned from migrant educators in every state was the value of treating every child with respect for their culture, their language, and their parents' work. Part of this work required that I get curious and actively listen, honor, and respect the personal stories and needs of each child and family I engaged. This involved making sure that each migrant child felt comfortable in a new school and had supporting adults who were always available for advice and protection. The migrant education programs essentially created belonging for millions of children in schools across the United States.

For me, the epitome of the migrant education program was when I heard a former migrant student testify before the Education and Labor Committee of the United States Senate about the consideration given to her and all migrant children by migrant educators. The atmosphere of belonging is what permitted so many within the program to flourish academically and socially. These children were made to feel respected, affirmed, and valued as they were.

These ideals align with much of what Rhodes shares in support of diversity, equity, and inclusion workplace commitments. I am convinced that the idea of belonging works. I know from my experience in migrant education that it takes hard work and complete dedication by all the teachers and administrators to support these commitments and practice acceptance. Rhodes argues that the same type of unified effort is necessary to achieve a sense of belonging at work.

In reading Rhodes' book, you will gain an understanding of what it means to truly belong at work. You will be able to imagine both how it feels not to belong and how it feels to belong. You will realize the full benefits to an organization for everyone in the workforce to feel they can be and act as their authentic selves.

Rhodes argues that an organization where full belonging has been achieved will benefit by greater individual contributions and an innovative atmosphere that will create prosperity for the organization, and therefore enhance its community. The alternative of not creating belonging, says Rhodes, will mean the organization will be at a competitive disadvantage, which will lead to failure in the long term. The evidence, logic, and passion that Rhodes provides advances this argument, and will likely compel you to take action.

Rhodes provides practical strategies you can take to help foster a feeling of belonging for your people. He details how to bring along colleagues who do not sense the need for change or the importance of belonging. He gives the means to convince even the most recalcitrant managers and supervisors of the need to change.

This book gives everyone a place to start. With a thoughtful reading of Rhodes' suggestions and practical actions, your organization has the potential to develop a diverse, equitable, and inclusive workforce that everyone deserves.

John Perry.

John Perry
Former New York State Senator

PREFACE

> **❝** *Much of what human beings do is done in the service of belongingness.* **❞**
> – Roy F. Baumeister[1]

When I think of what it means to belong at work, I'm reminded of a brilliant career advisor who offered mentorship toward the end of my graduate school days at the New York University Wagner School of Public Service. As I considered job opportunities in the public sector, he encouraged me to answer three key questions: 1) can I do the job, 2) will I do the job, and 3) do I *fit?* Empowered with these questions, I learned how to interview employers while they were evaluating me. As I considered many exciting opportunities in New York City, Washington, DC, and beyond, the first two questions were often answered with a solid YES. Yet, being a ***transgender**** job applicant in the early aughts made the answer to the third question *almost* always a painful NO.

When I began my career nearly two decades ago in the public sector, many organizations I considered lacked the knowledge, skills, and motivation to create an inclusive culture where I knew I would fit in; a culture where I knew I could *belong*. For context, the majority of organizations at that time lacked basic non-discrimination protections for transgender employees, making many of us, especially transgender people of color, vulnerable to being fired, denied a promotion, or even limited in the opportunity to be considered for employment simply because of who we are. As a result, I had to ***cover***, or censor, aspects of my ***gender identity*** to access gainful employment.

---

*For bold italic terms, please refer to the glossary located on page 129.

Covering during a job search meant that I had to downplay and disassociate my professional self from my *gender history*, and the rich experiences that shaped a large part of who I am in the world. I felt pressure to cover important associations with campus LGBTQ advocacy groups and campaigns I led in which we advocated for basic protections for LGBTQ students, faculty, and staff at New York University and the University of Notre Dame – much of my advocacy was honored through prestigious campus and community awards. My advocacy refined valuable transferable skills that I would have shared during my job search, had I felt prospective employers valued these associations, experiences, and skills.

During my job search, I understood that I would be required to surrender some aspects of my personal expression to align with a prospective employer's mission and values. For example, because it was not relevant to most of the jobs I applied for, I excluded my obsession with long-distance bicycle touring as a topic of conversation. Yet, when I arrived for interviews with prospective employers, I felt pressure to *improperly* cover defining aspects of who I am because of the signals I was picking up about the workplace culture. Going back to the question of "do I fit," the feeling of belonging felt nearly impossible when being interviewed by prospective employers.

The pressure to cover, or censor, core aspects of gender identity and political associations goes far beyond the experiences of transgender people like me. One study found 75% of employees cover things like their faith or Veteran status, alter their appearance such as covering up tattoos or piercings, or do not mention associations like having – or planning – a family.[2] Workplace covering is pervasive and negatively impacts individuals and organizations around the world. At the root of covering is something central to what we will explore in this book. When we place a veil over aspects of who we are, we assume that we are not good enough as we are, and that we must alter important aspects of our authentic selves in order to 'fit in," and gain employment.

My experiences of searching for a job after graduate school underscore this sense of not belonging. After several key interviews, I secured a job working for the White House Office of Management and Budget. The job was an incredible experience, and I found the work very rewarding. However, something was off. I experienced stress the majority of the time, and it didn't come from the workload, the high demands, or the responsibility of overseeing an annual operating budget of $11 billion. My stress derived from constantly having to place a veil over my authentic self. Namely, I withheld sharing that I was *assigned female at birth*, and covered important aspects of my gender history, as they were relevant to particular conversations.

I feared sharing my gender history for a number of reasons:

1. I was primarily afraid that I would be fired, as there were no existing non-discrimination protections for transgender employees at the time.
2. I feared my work would be unfairly judged, or that I would limit my potential for future promotions.
3. I was overwhelmed with the prospect of having to explain myself to my co-workers *again...and again...and again.*

This last fear arose because I assumed I was probably the first transgender person my colleagues would have ever met. At the time, it was estimated that less than 8% of adults in the United States knew or worked with a transgender person.[3] I often debated about coming out, especially when trying to bond with fellow colleagues about my past – it's challenging not to talk about childhood memories while traveling on site visits across the country, or simply while catching up at the water cooler.

So, like so many transgender employees still do today, I purposefully omitted aspects of my gender history from relevant conversations about childhood pastimes. The veil I placed over my authentic self was a valiant attempt to fit into the *dominant workplace culture* of *straight* and *cisgender* employees. I thought these actions would enable me to keep my head down, do quality work, and ascend the ranks of the White House career staff based on my merit, which would clearly demonstrate how much I belonged at work. I attempted to be an indispensable part of the team, which I thought would compel my colleagues to recognize how much I fit in.

I failed, and here is what I learned from trying to force myself into a culture that simply wasn't *yet* ready for me. I learned that covering important aspects of myself in order to fit into the White House culture had real costs. It cost me countless hours stressing out about things that had nothing to do with my work, and ultimately, limited my productivity on the job. It cost me the opportunity to truly bring my authentic self to work and celebrate who I am with my colleagues, which would have improved my relationships and ability to connect with those on my team. I am certain the energy I invested in managing this stress established barriers to cultivating true team morale and support.

Ultimately, I left the White House. The costs of staying and dealing with the anxiety and pressure to veil my authentic self was simply too much to bear. Working for an employer that failed to offer basic employee protections for me jeopardized my job security. I was constantly fearful of being outed, which could have resulted in losing my job. Such fears took a toll on my health and well-being. As a seasoned LGBTQ advocate, I felt shame for not being authentic in the workplace and making the efforts to improve the environment for other transgender employees. I knew I had the potential to make things better and realized that I would need to seek out greener pastures to ensure that my skills aligned with my life's purpose.

While much has happened in my career between leaving the White House and writing this book, my experience of not fitting in during this period of my life motivated me to become a diversity, equity, and inclusion professional. I knew I had the experience and skills to support executives, HR, and diversity professionals cultivate workplaces where all stakeholders know they belong. My intersectional approach to considering the perspectives of **underrepresented groups** was gleaned from years of advocating for communities living at the margins, including transgender and nonbinary people. These experiences enabled me to offer solutions for leaders struggling with how to implement their inclusion commitments into every everyday practice across their organizations. It also inspired me to write this book.

The pages ahead serve as a resource for leaders – and those on their way to joining them – to understand why cultivating a sense of belonging for all stakeholders can help advance the organization's mission. When employees know they can be their authentic selves at work – where their differences are recognized, accepted, and celebrated, and there's no pressure to assimilate – that's when employers will begin to leverage the true power of their people. Together, let's explore what it means to belong, understand why it matters, and gain the confidence to model it within our everyday workplace practices.

INTRODUCTION

❝ The idea of belonging shouldn't be considered a privilege available to only some. It should be considered a basic human right. ❞
– Linda Mullen, Executive Director of the Sparkle Effect[†]

Congratulations! You are reading this book because you recognize the value in transforming your organization into one that is more reflective and inclusive of everyone within your ***workplace ecosystem***. You have already taken steps toward an important commitment of familiarizing yourself with what is required to create a healthier workplace culture. Together, we will begin a journey to discover how to cultivate a *feeling of belonging* for your organization's most valuable asset, your people.

This book is designed for anyone who considers themselves a ***champion*** of diversity, equity, and inclusion (DEI) principles. It is also written for those aspiring champions ready to take their DEI practices to the next level with the goal of cultivating inclusive workplace cultures where everyone on the team feels valued and knows that they belong. Readers seeking inspiration and guidance to move their leadership team to implement their DEI commitments into everyday actions will confidently walk away with practical, inclusive leadership strategies after reading this book.

As you read, remember the times when you too have felt like you didn't belong at work, or where you found yourself placing a veil over core aspects of your authentic self in an effort to fit into your organization's culture. Reflect and consider these feelings, and work towards cultivating ***empathy*** with the content featured in this book. Your empathy and compassion will only deepen your commitment to taking meaningful actions, helping you build a more inclusive workplace.

ABOUT THIS BOOK

This book is divided into three main parts with the first breaking down the basics of what it means to cultivate a workplace culture of belonging. This section will unpack loaded diversity terminology that can sometimes be confusing. It will explore why humans have an innate need to belong. After reading part one, you will have a better understanding as to how the need to belong shows up in the workplace. Throughout the book, and especially this first section, pay particular attention to the italicized words and phrases in boldface. If you are unfamiliar with them, please reference the glossary section at the end of the book.

Part two will help you make the case to your organization's leaders as to why they must prioritize cultivating a workplace culture of belonging. Even if you are a seasoned DEI practitioner, you are encouraged to carefully read through this section. It features some of the latest research and case studies that will support you in making a persuasive business case helping you amplify the human imperative for committing to this work. Understanding both of these perspectives will allow you to inspire any audience, no matter if they are champions or *resisters* to workplace change. If you need more research to build your case for various audiences, you can locate all sources cited throughout this book in the *Notes* section located at the end of the book.

The third and final part of the book breaks down how you can build a workplace culture of belonging, regardless of your role. This section explains what an *inclusive leader* is, and how to determine if you have what it takes to bring about the workplace changes you desire. You will then have the opportunity to assess different actions you can take in your everyday practice to become an inclusive leader. The last chapter of the book offers coaching on how you can plan and implement short-term and long-term actions that will transform yourself and your organization. You will also receive guidance on how to hold yourself accountable to your personal and organizational commitments.

Each chapter begins with a quote inspiring you to take action and at the conclusion of every chapter, you'll find a short summary highlighting key points you can reference after you finish reading. This is followed by a short exercise designed to apply what you have learned into your daily job responsibilities. As you read along, you are encouraged to write in this book, underline talking points that resonate with your experiences, and use this book as a general roadmap to help your organization begin, or enhance, the journey of creating an inclusive workplace.

To extend the depth of knowledge available to you, the wisdom of six award-winning DEI thought leaders from across the United States is stitched within the fabric of this book. These thought leaders will share their take on some of the key themes presented. You can find their perspectives featured at the end of each chapter. These thought leaders include:

Thought leaders include:

1. Kylar Broadus, Esq., Global Human Rights Activist, Lawyer, Business Law Professor
2. Jennifer Brown, President & CEO, Jennifer Brown Consulting and Best-Selling Author, *Inclusion: Diversity, the New Workplace & the Will to Change*
3. Joel Brown, Ed.D., Chief Visionary Officer, Pneumos
4. Ashley Brundage, Vice President, Diversity & Inclusion, PNC Bank
5. Dre Domingue, Ed.D., Assistant Dean of Students for Diversity and Inclusion, Davidson College
6. Ben Duncan, Chief Diversity and Equity Officer, Multnomah County Office of Diversity and Equity

---

You can access the full thought leader interview audio files and written transcripts by visiting: **www.rhodesperry.com/belongingbook**, using the password **Belonging2018**. While you are on the website, you can also find digital worksheets, resources, and webinars related to the book's content. These worksheets serve as a tool to help you demonstrate and process all that you will learn as you read through the book. These digital resources also may be used with attribution to this book to help educate your colleagues on important concepts featured throughout.

Consider this book as your personal coach to help you stay focused on building an inclusive workplace fit for the twenty-first century. And like any good coach would recommend, let's begin our journey with a healthy warm-up.

TAKE THE PLEDGE!

As I work to become a more inclusive leader, I pledge to:

- **Make the Commitment.** I'll let my colleagues know I am reading this book with the goal of creating a feeling of belonging for employees, customers, and suppliers.
- **Serve as a *Possibility Model.*** I will serve as a champion of this work by treating others as they wish to be treated, and standing up for others, should they need an ally.
- **Share this Knowledge.** Once I have finished reading this book, I will share the ideas it offers with a friend or trusted colleague and encourage them to commit to this important work.

_____

Signature (First, Last Name)   Date (Month, Day, Year)

PART I

WHAT IT MEANS TO BELONG

UNDERSTANDING DIVERSITY TERMINOLOGY

&& *Kindness is a language that the deaf*
can hear and the blind can see. 55
– Mark Twain

DIVERSITY ≠ INCLUSION ≠ EQUITY

To understand what it means to belong, we must first level-set, or clarify, diversity, equity, and inclusion (DEI) terminology. Understanding diversity terminology is paramount given that a good number of individuals incorrectly use these terms. For example, when prospective clients request my consulting services, they often use the terms "diversity," "inclusion," or "equity" interchangeably. While I understand a prospective client's general goal to build a workplace culture of belonging, I'm not always clear as to the work they've done in the past based upon how they use these terms.

In this spirit, let's establish a foundation of what these terms mean in the context of the workplace. You will be the head of the class if you remember that diversity, equity, and inclusion are *not* synonyms. ***Diversity*** exists at work when the environment includes a variety of individuals, groups, and/or communities with different social and cultural characteristics, working styles, ideas, and experiences. Remember that cultivating a diverse workplace is not the destination. Rather, it is often an entry point to creating dynamic, innovative, and productive organizations.

Taking this work to an intermediate level involves introducing the concept of ***inclusion***. Inclusion in the workplace boils down to welcoming, respecting, supporting, and valuing the authentic participation of any individual or group. Executives from leading organizations understand the value proposition of engaging diverse people, ideas, and experiences throughout the organization. As a result, these organizations continue to lead as they introduce new methods designed to leverage the full potential of staff from across the organization. This form of engagement recognizes each individual employee for their valuable contributions and builds a sense of cooperation informing key decisions.

Rather than aspiring to build diverse and inclusive workplaces, I encourage my clients to establish equitable organizations. *Equity* in the workplace is rooted in the fair treatment, access, opportunity, and advancement of an employee while simultaneously attempting to identify and eliminate structural barriers that have prevented the full participation of underrepresented groups. Underrepresented groups consist of those people from identity groups that endure disadvantages in the workplace due to historical oppression and exploitation. An Oregon-based company, *Dave's Killer Bread*, offers an example of one way to foster equity at work for underrepresented groups. The company offers *second chance employment*, or the hiring of people with criminal backgrounds.

According to the company's founder, Dave Dahl, the deciding factor in whether someone with a criminal background will break through to a new life or return to criminal activity comes down to having access to employment with a livable wage and real career advancement opportunities.[5] Employers like *Dave's Killer Bread* offer a concrete example of how second chance employment can be implemented, helping a business thrive while eliminating systemic barriers for underrepresented groups in the workplace. After a decade of hiring people with criminal backgrounds, the company has produced the top selling organic bread in the nation where every 1 out of 3 employees on staff has a criminal background.

Equity ≠ Equality

Equity does not equal equality. When implemented effectively, equitable business practices actively work to dismantle structural barriers, such as bias, to hiring employees with criminal backgrounds. *Equality*, on the other hand, centers around the uniform distribution of resources and opportunities. Many assume promoting equality assures fairness. In reality, equality assures unequal advantages to those who already have competitive advantages over others, and they may not necessarily need the same level of support as another individual.

Equality ≠ Equity

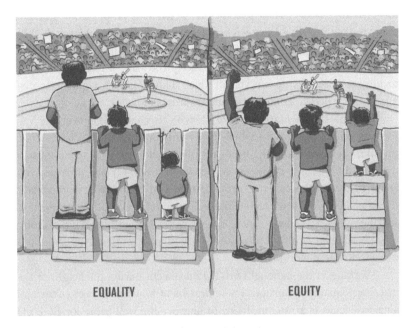

Figure 1.1[6]

For example, take a close look at Figure 1.1. On the left side of the image, every individual has equal access to resources (in this case a crate) with the goal of looking over the fence to view a baseball game. Even with equal access to the same resources, the shortest person does not have the same advantages as the tallest person, contributing to further inequities. In this instance, height is either the advantage or disadvantage allowing spectators to view the game.

On the right side of the image, the structural barrier of the fence preventing the full participation of the shortest person to view the baseball game without obstruction is eliminated when there is a reallocation of resources to ensure that all of the fans can fully view the game. Note the reallocation of resources is not a *zero-sum game*, meaning that when the tallest person gives up his crate to give a boost to the shortest person, the tallest person does not lose out on the experience to watch the game. When we commit to building an equitable workplace, we must understand that different people will need different resources to be treated fairly.

In this sense, we embrace the platinum rule over the golden rule. The **golden rule** encourages you to treat others the way in which *you* want to be treated. Sadly, when it comes to welcoming people from different backgrounds and *lived experiences* from our own, the golden rule falls short when trying to build an inclusive workplace. Why? It assumes that other people want to be treated in exactly the same way that you want to be treated, implying we are all alike. This approach completely dismisses other people's different needs, desires, and hopes.

Fortunately, the **platinum rule** offers an alternative. It encourages you to treat others the way in which *they* want to be treated. While subtle, this shift in considering the needs of others before your own can mean a world of difference to those you encounter in the workplace, provided you consistently put this rule into action. At the end of the day, it is important to remember when you practice this rule, you recognize other people have specific needs. In order to make others feel seen and heard, considering these needs and working to meet them will go a long way to creating a more welcoming workplace.

Working in the national LGBTQ movement during the height of the marriage equality campaign, I saw first-hand how limited resources and a narrow focus of strategies failed to improve the well-being for LGBTQ people living at the margins – in particular LGBTQ people of color, transgender and non-binary people, immigrants, young people, and aging adults. From the time Massachusetts legalized same-sex marriage in 2004 through the Supreme Court's landmark *Obergefell v Hodges* decision in 2015, 87 transgender and non-binary people – almost exclusively women of color – were brutally murdered simply because of who they were.[7]

Clearly the principles of equity for the most vulnerable LGBTQ community members was not a central part of the marriage equality campaign. Engaging the movement's wealthiest and most influential stakeholders meant advocating for legal and policy changes that directly benefited their well-being. Going back to the illustration in Figure 1.1, this type of engagement was akin to giving the tallest fan on the left every single crate, leaving the shorter fans with nothing to improve their view of the game.

Bringing this example back to the workplace, when introducing changes to improve the outcomes for all stakeholders in the workplace, it is critical to have a universal goal while centering changes around those experiencing the greatest barriers to full engagement. This approach is what John A. Powell has defined as **targeted universalism**.[8] In the context of the workplace, in order to cultivate a sense of belonging for all, it is imperative to address some of the structural barriers to "fitting in" often endured by underrepresented groups. When you take the time to understand existing workplace barriers for these employees, you have the potential of positively impacting the overall workplace climate for everyone.

THE IMPORTANCE OF INTERSECTIONALITY

To honestly discuss what equity in the workplace is, and why we should aspire to dismantle structural barriers that constrain fostering a welcoming environment for all employees, we must first understand what *identity groups* are, and how *intersectionality* fits into the equation. An identity group is one where a particular group of people from a specific culture or community share a sense of belonging given their backgrounds, beliefs, experiences or a combination of these things. An identity group can relate to a person's self-identity, social group association, or one's psychological identity related to self-image.[9]

Based on our association with different identity groups, we may find ourselves aligning with a *dominant group*, or an *underrepresented group*. A dominant group is one that is advantaged and has superior resources and rights in society. An underrepresented group is one whose members are disadvantaged and subjected to unequal treatment by the dominant group. An underrepresented group may or may not regard themselves as recipients of collective discrimination. Often dominant groups experience what is known as *privilege*, or power and advantages derived from the historical *oppression* and exploitation of other identity groups.

Each of us belongs to a number of different identity groups, and therefore experience the concept of *intersectionality*. Intersectionality, as illustrated in Figure 1.2, means that all of us have multiple identities that intersect such as gender, race, sexual orientation, religious beliefs, ability, work styles, political views, etc. More often than not, our intersecting identities sometimes allow us to experience privilege, while at other times, they expose us to endure oppression. At all times, we should avoid reducing ourselves, or others, to any one aspect of our identities. We are a combination of our intersecting identities, which makes each of us authentically original rather than monoliths.

With respect to my identity, here's how different advantages and disadvantages manifest in my life. My race, ability, education, and *perceived* gender all position me in dominant groups when I enter most workplaces.

Intersectionality

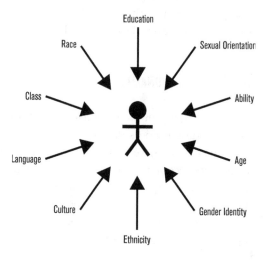

Figure 1.2[10]

This means as a white, able-bodied, educated, man, I am already afforded power and advantages over other people from different races, abilities, educational backgrounds, and genders. Yet, other aspects of my identity such as being introverted, bisexual, and transgender place me in underrepresented groups that endure disadvantages in the workplace. I may *cover* aspects of my identity if I believe they could adversely impact my job security.

COVERING IN THE WORKPLACE

Covering occurs when a person downplays or intentionally does not disclose a known stigmatized identity to fit in with the dominant culture. When it comes to the workplace, according to Kenji Yoshino, 61% of employees in the United States were found to cover some aspect of who they are at work.[11] When employees downplay their authentic selves, they negatively impact a workplace's overall productivity, innovation, and ability to build strong and meaningful relationships with fellow colleagues.

According to Yoshino's work, there are four ways covering manifests, as featured in Figure 1.3. The first includes altering personal appearance, including our grooming, hairstyles, mannerisms, or attire. While

Manifestations of Covering

APPEARANCE

 Employees may intentionally *change their self-expression* in order to fit in. This may include cutting off dreadlocks, wearing clothing to cover tattoos, or dressing in more traditionally masculine or feminine ways.

ADVOCACY

 Employees may be less likely to *speak about topics* central to their identities. This may include talking about politics, religion, military status, age, or other third rail workplace topics that may incite passion or bias.

AFFILIATION

 Employees may avoid *behaviors* associated with their identity groups to overcome stereotypes about that identity group. This may compel an aging employee to refrain from requesting time off to take care of their terminally ill partner, or a parent to limit their family leave to take care of their infant.

ASSOCIATION

 Employees may intentionally avoid socializing with other group members. For example, a bisexual employee may refrain from joining their organization's LGBTQ employee resource group for fear they will be outed, or a Muslim employee may avoid socializing with other people of faith for fear that they will be viewed as "too religious."

Figure 1.3[12]

still adhering to professional standards, some of us go out of our way to alter our authentic expression. This aspect of covering compels some of us to change our attire, such as a woman who conforms to the workplace's implicit culture of wearing skirts and make-up in order to blend in and get along with fellow colleagues when she would rather wear pants suits and no make-up in order to express a more authentic version of her gender.

The second aspect to covering occurs around affiliation based on our relationships. When it comes to family building, a person in a same-sex relationship may not disclose the gender of their partner. Similarly, a pregnant person or someone planning to adopt a child may withhold this information from their supervisor for fear of not earning a promotion or securing the stretch assignment that will enable them to develop professionally and advance within the organization.

Covering also occurs around advocacy, or our relationship to certain groups. Some Veterans, for example, will not disclose their military background, while others with different faith traditions may not disclose aspects of their spiritual practices. Somewhat related to this aspect of covering is when people downplay associations with certain people from underrepresented groups, such as a Veteran or a person from a different nationality, for fear of being associated with these underrepresented groups, and experiencing similar biases.

The Cultural Iceberg

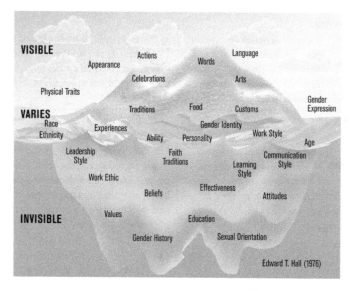

Figure 1.4[13]

YOUR CULTURAL ICEBERG

Understandably, there are things we can cover, and there are things we cannot cover in the workplace. Many DEI practitioners often use the visual of the cultural iceberg featured in Figure 1.4. This visual demonstrates what we can and cannot cover to our fellow colleagues. Things that are often difficult to cover include our visible presentation, including how we communicate, the clothing we wear to express our gender, the language we use, our mannerism, etc.

Based on our relationships with others, we may discuss aspects of our identities that we can cover, including our attitudes, opinions, personal values, and cultural assumptions. The aspects that are less visible, or not visible at all, help define us and our full self-expression. If we like, know, and trust our colleagues, we are more likely to lower our water line and express our sincere and authentic selves to them. Taking this action creates genuine connections with our colleagues and helps boost team morale leading to a more inclusive workplace.

We hold our core cultural values, assumptions, and *unconscious biases* at the deepest depths of our cultural icebergs. Unconscious biases are attitudes toward and stereotypes of other social groups that negatively affect our understanding, actions, and decisions in an unconscious way.[14] They impact everything we do, and when it comes to the workplace, they affect things like the employment cycle (i.e., hiring, firing, promotions, etc.), board selection, succession planning, conference speakers, and much more.

To gain self-awareness of both our superpowers and the areas where we need to grow, it is essential to understand where our unconscious biases live. To shine a light on these biases, we have effective tools at our fingertips, such as the Implicit Association Test (IAT).[15] Developed by Mahzarin Banaji and Anthony Greenwald, this tool enables a test-taker to explore the hidden biases that we all carry based on how we were socially conditioned to think about various identity groups based on their age, gender, race, ethnicity, religion, social class, sexual orientation, disability status, national origin, etc.[16]

Review the latest Equal Employment Opportunity Commission statistics and you'll quickly understand how unconscious biases in the workplace lead to expensive and preventable litigation caused from *microaggressions* and *discrimination* in the workplace.[17] A microaggression occurs when brief, everyday exchanges send denigrating messages to certain individuals because of their identity group membership.[18] Discrimination occurs when a person experiences overt, big actions based on prejudice that unfairly treats them differently because of, or punishes them for an aspect of their identity.[19]

When our unconscious biases go unchecked in the workplace, we may not intend to cause a microaggression or to discriminate against a fellow colleague, yet we must take full responsibility for how our actions *impact* another person or group. Our *intentions* are something that we *meant* to do, while our impact on another person or group of people includes the *effect* such actions had on them.

Think of intention versus impact as a physical concept. For example, say you were traveling to Hawaii to visit an old friend. As you arrive in the baggage claim area, you can see your friend running up with excitement to give you a big hug. In their haste, they accidentally step on your toe, shooting an electrical current of pain right up your leg. Immediately, your friend looks at you with deep concern and continues to apologize over-and-over saying that they didn't mean to hurt you. Their *intent* was to welcome you to Hawaii, yet, their *impact* left you with a broken toe, and a less than ideal vacation.

Now translate this physical concept into an emotional one. If a person or group of people express hurt or offense by your intentions, say for example you fail to use the correct pronouns for a staff person who has asked you to use gender neutral pronouns (i.e., they, them, theirs). While you may want to explain your intent, refrain from taking a defensive position. Remember only another person or group of people can determine the *impact* of your actions, words, or nonverbal cues. Instead of reacting, pause and deeply listen to what's being shared. Reflect on what you learned about the impact of your intentions, and identify ways you are working to become more aware of your unconscious biases.

Understanding the different identity groups and structural barriers some of these groups may endure in your workplace will empower you to become more **culturally responsive** to them. Greater understanding will help you become more aware of how your unconscious biases and best intentions may adversely create an unwelcoming environment for some stakeholders at work. When you take the time to self-educate and refine your language and decision making lens into one that is more culturally responsive, you are more likely to move towards building a more inclusive workplace culture.

Good news! You have made it through the most challenging part of the book. Now you have a better understanding of the basic terminology used throughout. Remember, this chapter offers the necessary foundation to begin cultivating more diverse and inclusive organizations. The next two chapters will help you understand what it means to belong, and why belonging matters in the workplace. Before we go there, check out a summary of the key points articulated in this chapter, and put your learnings into action by completing Exercise 2.

CHAPTER 1 – BELONGING BASICS

- ⊙ Diversity ≠ Inclusion ≠ Equity ≠ Equality.
- ⊙ Intersectionality can sometimes allow us to experience advantages, while at other times, exposes us to enduring disadvantages.
- ⊙ Covering negatively impacts 61% of the U.S. workforce and creates barriers to team morale, productivity, and innovation.
- ⊙ Unconscious bias impacts all aspects of our work. Great leaders do the work to gain awareness to understanding their unconscious biases and strive to overcome them.
- ⊙ Our good intentions are not an excuse for negative impacts that an individual or group brings to our attention.

EXERCISE 1:
TAKE THE QUIZ

Directions: Read each of the definitions and match them with the correct term. Hint, there will be one term left that does not have a matching definition.

A: Unconscious Bias	D: Identity Group	G: Intent	J: Privilege
B: Inclusion	E: Equality	H: Impact	K: Discrimination
C: Equity	F: Diversity	I: Covering	L: Microaggression
M: Intersectionality		N: Cultural Responsiveness	

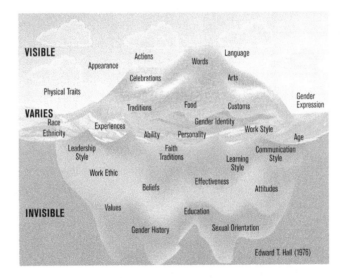

VISIBLE
Appearance Actions Words Language
Celebrations Arts
Physical Traits
Gender Expression
VARIES Traditions Food Customs
Race Experiences Gender Identity Work Style
Ethnicity Ability Personality Age
Leadership Style Faith Traditions Learning Style Communication Style
Work Ethic
Beliefs Effectiveness Attitudes
INVISIBLE Values Education
Gender History Sexual Orientation

Edward T. Hall (1976)

1.*   _F_   *An environment where a variety of different individu-*
    (Example)   *als, groups, and/or communities with different social and cultural characteristics exist.*

2.   _____   Cultivating an environment where any individual or group can be and feel welcomed, respected, supported, and valued to fully participate.

3.   _____   Fair treatment, access, opportunity, and advancement while simultaneously striving to identify and eliminate barriers that have prevented the full participation of some groups.

4. _____ Evenly distributed access to resources and opportunities necessary for a safe and healthy life; uniform distribution of access to ensure fairness.

5. _____ A particular group, culture, or community with which an individual identifies or shares a sense of belonging.

6. _____ Power and advantages benefiting a dominant identity group derived from the historical oppression and exploitation of other identity groups.

7. _____ Downplaying or intentionally not disclosing a known stigmatized identity to fit in with the dominant culture.

8. _____ Having multiple identities that intersect like gender, race, sexual orientation, which sometimes can offer privilege in some ways, but not in others.

9. _____ Overt, big actions based on prejudice that unfairly treat a person differently because of, or punish them for, an aspect of their identity.

10. _____ Attitudes toward and stereotypes of other social groups that negatively affect our understanding, actions, and decisions in an unconscious way.

11. _____ Brief, everyday exchanges that send denigrating messages to certain individuals because of their group membership.

12. _____ An action a person, group, or community *meant* to do.

13. _____ The *effect* an action had on a person, group, or community.

─────────────── **THOUGHT LEADER LESSONS** ───────────────

What is Your Take on Diversity, Equity, and Inclusion Language and Its Evolution in the Workplace?

❝ As diversity professionals, we have the challenge of building empathy with those we teach. By softening the words we use, and talking around hard concepts like oppression and all of the -isms that show up in the workplace, our audience can sometimes miss what we're talking about. And yet, we have to find new ways of building empathy and compel those we work with to make a commitment to this work. ❞

– Kylar Broadus, Global Human Rights Activist,
Lawyer, Business Law Professor

❝ I have this kind of terminology conversation all the time. Honestly, terminology changes every single day. I find it interesting as [different identity groups] have their own preference on acceptable terms. Connecting the dots between these different groups is key, and contributes to the rapidly changing terms. ❞

– Ashley Brundage, Vice President,
Diversity & Inclusion, PNC Bank

❝ I love the work that John Powell has been doing out of the Haas Center at Berkeley, and his frames of inclusion and belonging. John is trying to expand a sense of belonging through his concept of targeted universalism, or universal goals. His work talks about how everyone is a part of our concern. So we're not othering populations, we're actually expanding our circle of love – a concept that is a bold one in and of itself. ❞

– Ben Duncan, Chief Diversity and Equity Officer,
Multnomah County Office of Diversity and Equity

❝ Putting language to oppression is hard. Some thought leaders try to put language to it based on their own observations of what they experienced in the environment around them. When I think about the word diversity, it is a useful term to help us look at and appreciate our differences. While that's good to do, it's not enough because it doesn't help our systems evolve and change for the better. ❞

– Dre Domingue, Assistant Dean of Students for
Diversity and Inclusion, Davidson College

❝ I welcome the specificity that the really granular language that we have for things now allows everyone to feel seen and heard, and kind of known. Because when you put a name to something, for some of us, some kinds of names when they're not used in a derogatory sense, allows us to locate ourselves in the universe with more specificity. ❞

– Jennifer Brown, President & CEO, Jennifer Brown Consulting

❝ To talk about [diversity, equity, and inclusion] at work means that you're speaking truth to power. You're actually confronting patriarchy, you're confronting racism, you're confronting heterosexism. And as the old adage reads, the fox is not likely to concede the henhouse. ❞

– Joel Brown, Chief Visionary Officer, Pneumos

THE HUMAN NEED TO BELONG

> 66 *A deep sense of love and belonging is an irreducible need of all people. We are biologically, cognitively, physically, and spiritually wired to love, to be loved, and to belong. When those needs are not met, we don't function as we were meant to. We break. We fall apart. We numb. We ache. We hurt others. We get sick.* 99
> — Brene Brown[20]

MASLOW'S PYRAMID OF NEEDS

We need to belong. This human need ranks third among Maslow's iconic pyramid of needs as featured in Figure 2.1.[21] The need to belong ranks just

Maslow's Pyramid of Needs

Figure 2.1[22]

above our physiological need for food, water, and shelter, and our safety needs of personal security and well-being.[23] Maslow's work, complemented by emerging neuroscience research, indicates that the social need to belong "[is] managed using the same neural networks as used for primary survival needs such as food and water."[24] The neural networks in our brains constantly scan our environments to first assess our safety and then to determine if we fit.

"Do I belong?" Subconsciously, our brains ask this fundamental question each time our environment shifts, with the goal of determining our sense of belonging and the possible threat of rejection. As we assess an environment, our neural networks make judgements about the people we encounter. Our brains assess if these people fit within the "us" versus "them" paradigm. Such assessments help us determine if we belong, or if the people we encounter pose threats. When making these assessments, two key brain responses activate:

1. The threat response located in the limbic system, which regulates memory, decision making, and emotional response.
2. The reward response located in the prefrontal cortex and the posterior cingulate, which organizes our thoughts and actions aligned with our internal goals.[25]

When our brain determines that we do not belong or processes feelings of rejection from a particular person or group of people, our threat response activates in the limbic system. When this occurs, our brain

The Belonging Brain Anatomy

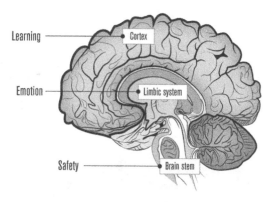

Learning — Cortex

Emotion — Limbic system

Safety — Brain stem

Figure 2.2[26]

processes these feelings in the same way as it processes physical pain, thirst, and hunger. Understandably, our brain activates its alarm system, sending the sympathetic nervous system, or our fight or flight response, into high gear. If our neural networks sense feelings of rejection or lack of belonging on a regular basis, we may compromise our immune system, experience inflammation, and exacerbate existing diseases such as cancer, diabetes, and those associated with aging.[27]

Conversely, when we know that we belong and experience feelings of acceptance from a particular person or group of people, our reward response activates in the prefrontal cortex. When this occurs, our brain processes feelings of acceptance in a similar way as it responds to a loving and supportive romantic partner. Research further confirms that when people respond to physically or emotionally painful situations in lab settings, viewing a picture of a loved one who gives them a sense of belonging helps to reduce the level of pain.[28] Such findings underscore the correlation between feeling a sense of belonging and experiencing good health.

THE LONELINESS EPIDEMIC

One might understandably assume that the average person experiences higher levels of social connection and feelings of belonging and acceptance in our modern world. Logically, this assumption makes sense, given the ease of engaging anyone from around the globe with access to an internet connection. At the touch of our fingertips, we can call our best friend who lives in Orlando from a beach in Costa Rica. We can connect with a nephew studying abroad in Hong Kong from our home in Missoula. Social media in particular offers a gateway to bridge the gap between real life relationships and digital communities located on Facebook, Instagram, YouTube, Twitter, LinkedIn and many other digital platforms.

Despite this level of global connectivity, mounting evidence suggests a rise of loneliness around the globe and across generations, threatening our health and well-being at alarming levels.[29] As academics and public health thought leaders grapple with these findings, a number of experts advocate for including loneliness on the list of public health concerns. Some people have taken matters into their own hands, forming charitable organizations like *The Loneliness Campaign*, which is designed to raise awareness and offer resources to respond to this growing challenge.[30]

So, why is loneliness and social isolation rising in an age when communications technology continues to rapidly improve? The influence loneliness has on social groups, coupled with the impacts it has on social media platforms, likely contributes to its rise. According to the General Social Survey, the number of respondents with "zero" close friends has tripled since 1985.[31] Research shows that loneliness acts as a contagion, meaning that when someone close in your life expresses that they feel lonely, you are 52% more likely to express a similar feeling.[32]

According to Dr. Nicholas A. Christakis, a sociologist and physician known for his research on social networks:

> *If you're lonely, you transmit loneliness, and then you cut the tie, or the other person cuts the tie. But now that person has been affected, and they proceed to behave the same way. There is this cascade of loneliness that causes a disintegration of the social network.*[33]

The contagion of loneliness becomes viral when fueled by the power of the internet. For example, if a friend on Facebook expresses feelings of loneliness, you are more likely to mirror similar feelings, which can then destabilize your entire online social network. Ironically, many of us often turn to the internet when we feel bored, isolated, anxious, or depressed.[34] We believe that our online relationships have the ability to substitute authentic and in-person connections. Online relationships result in superficial human connections and do not have the same positive health benefits as authentic offline ones.[35]

Research confirms that when we encounter a lonely person, we tend to drive them away. Socially isolating the loneliest people in our society further exacerbates this alarming epidemic. According to sociologist Phillip Slater's *Toilet Assumption*, coined in his book *The Pursuit of Loneliness*, we falsely assume that if we intentionally ignore undesirable feelings or emotions, they will disappear.[36] This assumption attempts to "deny the reality of human interdependence," and our fundamental need to belong by receiving social acceptance. The rise of our online "friendships" and social media followers demonstrates our aversion to feeling lonely and deluding ourselves into feeling a false sense of belonging.

THE POWER OF BELONGING

When we feel an authentic sense of belonging, our interests, motivation to learn new things, health, and happiness improve. Belonging in a group advances our position on Maslow's Pyramid of needs. Our intellectual achievement, immune function, and overall well-being also improve, and we are more motivated to overcome obstacles. This increased motivation helps us identify problems and innovate solutions, opening up new options, experiences, and ideas to tackle long standing challenges in our lives.

To address the rising tide of social loneliness and cultivate a sense of belonging, social psychologist Greg Walton developed the Social-Belonging Intervention.[37] While initially developed for first year college students who felt that they didn't fit in on campus, Walton came up with a framework that can be applied in a variety of settings, including the workplace. According to Walton, the framework consists of two broad messages:

1) If you feel like you don't belong…, you (and other people like you) are not alone.
2) If you feel this way, your experience will improve over time.[38]

Putting this framework into practice required juniors and seniors on campus to be trained to connect with first year students who were struggling with "fitting in." They accomplished this work by sharing quotations, statistics, and stories of similar times when they felt that they didn't belong, but eventually overcame these feelings. The approach helped first year students understand that no matter how isolated they felt, those feelings were common and were not evidence that they didn't belong. Rather, they were encouraged to recognize the opportunity to grow and to see that over time, they were likely to feel a greater sense of belonging.

This intervention also had a positive impact on overcoming gender and racial *achievement gaps* for women and students of color in overwhelmingly white and male-dominated majors. Given the realities of racism and sexism on campuses in the United States, women and students of color often attribute challenging circumstances to feelings of not belonging because of their race or gender. Walton's research demonstrated that the Social-Belonging Intervention delivered in the first year of college shifted the perspectives and academic trajectory of these students, improving their overall grade-point average and reducing the achievement gap by 50%.[39]

The success of the Social-Belonging Intervention in academic environments may prove to offer powerful results in other settings, such as the workplace. The power of the intervention enables recipients to transform their perceptions of belonging or not belonging. When considering the good and bad things that occur every day, those trained in the intervention are less likely to interpret bad days with not belonging, given the intervention's guidance to help understand that daily struggles are normal and a healthy aspect to being human.

BELONGING AT WORK

Let us now consider how we can adapt the Social-Belonging Intervention into the workplace. It has the power to help transform our organizations into ones where more of our colleagues can gain a better sense of belonging. According to Walton's research, when delivering the two broad messages of the Social-Belonging Intervention outlined above, the following four approaches may help you determine how to apply this concept into the workplace:

1. **Acknowledge Their Feelings.** When a colleague expresses to you that they feel as if they don't fit in at work, first acknowledge their feelings. You can do this by giving your complete attention to them, deeply listening, and summarizing their difficulties after they have finished speaking. This form of active listening helps signal to your colleague that you have listened to their struggles, and that you have taken the time to acknowledge their challenges. Most importantly, giving your attention to them demonstrates your willingness to offer support. Don't try to problem solve or tell them what you would do. Just bear witness to their challenges by listening.

2. **Strength in Numbers.** Normalize their struggles by reminding them that they aren't alone. There is strength in numbers, and you may want to remind your colleague how others have been in a similar place. If your colleague views their struggles as something that aren't likely to change, validate them, and pivot by sharing how these challenges will not get in their way to succeeding in their role. Acknowledge their challenges, and let them know there are always ways to work around them when they are ready. Let them know you are available to explore those options, and offer support when these feelings arise.

3. **Share Your Story.** Share a story of a time where you felt as if you didn't belong at work. When sharing your story, consider offering one aspect of being vulnerable on the job. For example, if a colleague is struggling with sharing that she's planning to a have a child, and worries that the office isn't family friendly, consider coming out to her about your experiences with struggling to put a picture on your desk of your same sex partner, and connect with her about your worry that the office wasn't overtly LGBTQ friendly. When you make connections, and share more about the company's values and culture, you may have a breakthrough.

4. **The Answers are Within.** Encourage your colleague to trust their intuition and inner wisdom when navigating the challenges at hand. Using a strengths-based approach, ask your colleague if they have encountered similar challenges in the past, and if so, encourage them to share the strategies they used to resolve the matter. Before offering HR resources to support your colleague, explore how you and other colleagues can show up to support in informal ways. By connecting in this manner, you're helping foster a sense of belonging in the workplace.

CHAPTER 2 - BELONGING BASICS

- Belonging is a fundamental human need.
- The feeling of isolation is akin to physical pain, hunger, and thirst.
- The rise of the internet, and predominantly social media platforms, have contributed to the epidemic of loneliness.
- The feeling of belonging increases our intellectual achievement, immune function, and overall well-being.
- The Social-Belonging Intervention offers strategies to overcome feelings of loneliness in the workplace.

EXERCISE 2:
REFLECT ON YOUR WORKPLACE EXPERIENCES

Directions: Think of a time when you felt different from everyone else at work. For example, walking into a meeting you may have found yourself being the only person from a different race, or the only woman, or the only person who spoke English, or the only Veteran, etc. Spend some time reflecting on the following questions, and then write your answers in the fields below.

REFLECTION QUESTIONS:

1. Describe a workplace situation where you felt different from everyone else on the job. Write down two or three sentences detailing the context and what was taking place.

    _____

    _____

    _____

2. Who was in the room that made you feel different? What did you perceive the group having in common that you did not share with them?

    _____

    _____

    _____

3. Write all of the emotions associated with feeling different. Spend some time and get specific as to what was taking place that brought these feelings up for you?

    _____

    _____

    _____

4. Based on the feelings you described above, what is one word that best summarizes what you felt in this particular workplace scenario?

    _____

    _____

    _____

5. How did the experience you described above impact your job performance and overall experiences at this particular organization?

    _____

    _____

    _____

──────────── **THOUGHT LEADER LESSONS** ────────────

Is there a role for the workplace to disrupt the epidemic of loneliness?

❝ Isolation has been a public health construct for a long time. As we continue to implement our workforce equity strategy, the need for peer-to-peer support shows up so much. People want to be, and are hungry for more meaningful connections with people they work with every day, and that shows up in so many different aspects of the work. When we recognize how important this feeling is, we need to further explore how to keep moving it into our organizations. ❞

– Ben Duncan, Chief Diversity and Equity Officer,
Multnomah County Office of Diversity and Equity

❝ I think that's why we have all of these diversity and inclusion programs, to enact opportunities for people to really connect with other employees. In my role, I'm not only connecting with employees, but I'm connecting with the community and customers. Every day includes constant interactions, and I see the challenges so many of my colleagues have working in a role where they don't have that level of interaction. ❞

– Ashley Brundage, Vice President of
Diversity & Inclusion, PNC Bank

❝ Virtualization of a lot of our jobs has really, really helped with diversity and inclusion, honestly. It's meant that so many people that would have left jobs and employment, no longer need to leave. It's like they can have their family and their job and their work, and they can manage it themselves. That's beautiful, and that's been something that has…the value of that in particular, has been important for women and for parents, and for anybody who's 'nontraditional'...there is a flip side, and the risk of disconnection is very real. **"**

– Jennifer Brown, President & CEO, Jennifer Brown Consulting

" I see many people having a lack of purpose. When you don't have a sense of purpose, then you feel lost...part of loneliness to me is just a subset of alienation, and alienation can occur with yourself, it can occur in terms of how you see yourself as a global citizen, in terms of how you see yourself spiritually. I think in that aspect, work has a really critical role, because work, at least I hope, should afford you some sense of purpose and some sense of dignity. **"**

– Joel Brown, Chief Visionary Officer, Pneumos

" The pace of life and the pace of work is so quick these days. [In the workplace] there's not a time to develop that relationship... leaders have to recognize the challenges of our current society [with respect to loneliness] by encouraging face-to-face dialogue, and slowing down. **"**

– Dre Domingue, Assistant Dean of Students for
Diversity and Inclusion, Davidson College

" Some workplace policies we are seeing around family medical leave and pay equity are helpful, but they are government-led. Given the current political gridlock, I think this is where corporations need to step up and allow that space. When that happens, I think we'll get somewhere. **"**

– Kylar Broadus, Global Human Rights Activist,
Lawyer, Business Law Professor

THE IMPORTANCE OF BELONGING AT WORK

❝ I've learned that people will forget what you said, people will forget what you did, but people will never forget how you made them feel. ❞
– Maya Angelou

DISRUPTING LONELINESS AT WORK

The workplace has the power to connect all of us in an authentic and meaningful way. Our relationships with our colleagues and other stakeholders in the workplace ground this powerful connection. Everything from formal team meetings to brainstorming sessions to passing conversations in the hallways can stimulate creativity and our ability to polish ideas through our relationships. When we intentionally design our workplace to foster a greater sense of team morale and camaraderie, we have the ability to disrupt the hazards of loneliness and to unleash our organization's potential.

Unfortunately, the workplace is not a panacea to combat the contagion of loneliness. In fact, the need to belong at work is often overlooked by executives and other business leaders. Based on my experience with organizational change, when employers focus efforts on executing new policies, programs, systems, or ideas, the concept of facilitating connections and stronger teams is almost always an afterthought, if not neglected altogether. As a result, our employees often feel alienated from their colleagues and disconnected from their work.[40] Their sense of contribution declines, and so does their productivity.

When employees feel disconnected from their colleagues, they often feel the need to veil important aspects of their authentic selves in order to protect their job security. As we discussed in Chapter 1, 61% of employees cover at work, limiting their full expression of self and the people and groups they associate with in their daily lives.[41] Censoring aspects of yourself on the job creates unnecessary interpersonal barriers, which ultimately compromises the ability to develop meaningful professional relationships. It also spreads the contagion of loneliness across the workplace.

THE IMPACTS OF LONELINESS AT WORK

When we consider those most impacted by the loneliness epidemic at work, we discover virtually everyone on the job is adversely affected. Groups that are historically underrepresented in the workplace cover at higher rates. According to Kenji Yoshino and Christie Smith's *Uncovering Talent* whitepaper, 83% of LGBTQ people, 79% of Black people, 67% of women of color, 66% of all women, and 63% of Latinx people censor important aspects of themselves on the job.[42] The pressure of conforming to a workplace culture also has an adverse impact on enfranchised groups in the workplace with 45% of white, straight, cisgender men also censoring important aspects of themselves on the job.[43]

Covering, or limiting our full self-expression on the job, combined with *minority stress*, creates significant barriers for underrepresented groups in the workplace. Minority stress describes the chronically high levels of stress endured by members of these groups in society, often caused by interpersonal or organizational *microaggressions* and *discrimination*.[44] Microaggressions are brief, everyday exchanges that send denigrating messages to certain individuals because of their group membership, while workplace discrimination often involves overt actions based on prejudice that unfairly treats a person differently, or punishes them for an aspect of their identity. The psychological costs of these dynamics in the workplace shave off years of the life expectancy of employees from underrepresented groups, especially employees of color.[45]

The following excerpt from an Atlantic Magazine article entitled, *Being Black – but Not Too Black – in the Workplace* amplifies how minority stress coupled with covering can undermine efforts to cultivate a sense of belonging at work:

> ...*while everyone needs to create and put forth an "appropriate" workplace identity, for members of minority groups—women of all races, racial-minority men, LGBTQ people—this becomes particularly taxing*

*because their working identities must counter common cultural stereo-
types. For example, black men may feel compelled to work longer hours
as a way to repudiate stereotypes of a poor work ethic among blacks.
To make matters more complicated, such strategies can backfire, rein-
forcing other stereotypes: Working those long hours may lead colleagues
to assume that the workers lack the intellectual preparation needed for
high-status professional jobs.*[46]

Stereotype threat, or the situation where people believe they are
at risk of confirming stereotypes about the identity groups they belong
to, exacerbate the levels of minority stress underrepresented groups in
the workplace endure.[47] Underrepresented groups are far more likely to
endure the negative impacts of minority stress. As a result, they are more
likely to cover aspects of their identity that aren't visible when negative
stereotypes about their identity groups are present in the workplace. For
example, if a gay employee who is not out to his colleagues overhears a fellow employee saying negative things about LGBTQ people, he experiences
a microaggression and will likely endure higher levels of minority stress.
Such stress triggers his instinct to censor important aspects about himself
and his family to protect his job security.

While minority stress does not impact the most enfranchised employees, the pressure to conform to the workplace's culture does take its toll
on them. For example, a straight, white, cisgender, male executive being
considered for a significant promotion decides to cover his family association. He and his spouse are expecting a new child in a few months, and
he refrains from sharing this exciting news for fear that the promotion
won't happen. He makes this decision because he remembered how a former colleague was overlooked for a similar promotion because his spouse
was expecting a baby. Imagine the stress of withholding such life changing
news from the people you spend the majority of your day with, and how it
would adversely impact your job performance.

CREATING AN INTENTIONAL CULTURE

Even when a workplace effectively communicates the importance of its
diversity, equity, and inclusion (DEI) values, employees may still feel pres-
sured to conform to the organization's culture. This pressure to assimilate
occurs when a workplace's values fail to translate into measurable, daily

practices. The consequences leave both dominant and underrepresented groups with a feeling of not belonging or "fitting in" with the organization's *implicit culture*. When an organization overlooks the importance of aligning and informing its DEI values, beliefs, and commitments in support of the overall mission or business strategy, it is left with an unfocused, or implicit workplace culture that usually benefits only the most enfranchised leaders.

To understand why aligning your business strategy with your workplace's DEI values matters, let's unpack what an organization's values include. The values of your workplace consist of a set of explicitly defined organizational principles, informed by key stakeholders throughout the workplace. An organization's values guide key decision making and the overall business strategy. Your values offer a framework to determine the socially responsible, or "right" action to take, even when faced with extraordinarily difficult choices. Workplaces that carry B Corporation Certificates offer concrete examples of how to align your organization's values with the mission.[48]

Ben & Jerry's, a Certified B Corporation, offers a helpful example of how the business publicly shares its values around social and environmental responsibility to its customers. Ben & Jerry's publicly shares its vision for corporate social responsibility through embracing fair trade practices to be better stewards of the planet, and through their commitment to invest in the community through supporting community-based projects. The company also champions corporate *social responsibility* for its employees by implementing a livable wage policy, creating a better work-life balance for employees, championing their health, and cultivating a sustainable supply chain.[49]

Alternatively, when a company fails to align its decision making process with its values, an implicit culture arises. Implicit cultural norms include undefined and hard to express features of what it *feels* like to work within a particular workplace. When workplace values are not defined, communicated, understood, and championed by employees at all levels of the organization, individual employees create disparate cultures within the broader organization. Micro-cultures bubble up throughout the organization, and thrive in especially large multinational corporations and government agencies.

With the absence of clearly defined workplace values, implicit culture takes root, further distancing you from the goal of fostering a feeling of belonging at work. For example, I once worked with a colleague who was faced with a tough decision. She had to choose between two equally qualified candidates for a senior level position that would be interfacing with a number of publicly elected officials. When I talked with her about how she was going to make the final decision, she shared that it would be easy, as she was going to pick the candidate that best "fit" within the workplace culture. In this instance, the more introverted candidate was overlooked, because my colleague believed "extroverts thrive in most workplaces."

To fully understand this example, there are a few factors to consider about this particular workplace culture. First, it was a municipal government agency that still needed to clearly articulate what its DEI values were and how they informed business decisions like hiring practices. In the absence of these values, hiring managers were left with a standard non-discrimination policy, and their own interpretations of what this policy meant with respect to creating a more inclusive work environment. When my colleague reflected on the workplace culture, she clearly said one of the implicit requirements was the ability to fit in with fellow extroverts, whereas from my experience as an introvert, I saw the value and strength in mixing up the leadership team with different personalities, workstyles, and perspectives.[50]

This example illustrates how implicit culture often obscures a hiring manager's **unconscious biases** by overlooking qualified candidates that don't look, think, work, or offer similar experiences to those people already on the team. Not surprising, when relying on "cultural fit" to make a hiring decision when your organization has yet to establish an **intentional culture**, a workplace runs the risk of engaging in **groupthink**. Group think leads to homogeneity, which can jeopardize a workplace's relevance as a thriving business in the twenty-first century. Veiling our unconscious biases behind "culture fit" is something we must work to overcome. We can hold our unconscious biases accountable by thoughtfully defining our DEI values, and relying upon them when making important decisions like hiring a new employee.

A workplace's values serve as the foundation of how the business operates in the world. Some businesses literally etch these values into marble because they are timeless and essential as illustrated in Figure 3.1 below. At the same time, if your workplace has already gone through the important process of creating stakeholder informed values, it is essential that every stated value incorporates a diversity, equity, and inclusion lens. Remember that this lens offers the bridge to cultivating a feeling a belonging, and if you haven't yet taken this step, chances are, many employees aren't engaged in their everyday functions. Even more troubling, when an employee feels as if they don't fit in, they often seek greener pastures.

Ned Space Code of Conduct

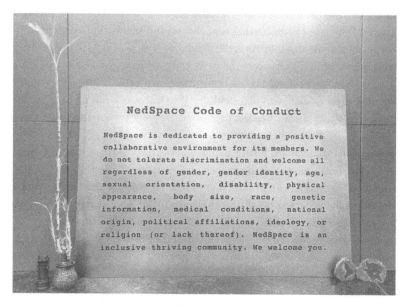

NedSpace Code of Conduct

NedSpace is dedicated to providing a positive collaborative environment for its members. We do not tolerate discrimination and welcome all regardless of gender, gender identity, age, sexual orientation, disability, physical appearance, body size, race, genetic information, medical conditions, national origin, political affiliations, ideology, or religion (or lack thereof). NedSpace is an inclusive thriving community. We welcome you.

Figure 3.1[51]

INFORMING DECISIONS WITH A DEI LENS

So, what exactly is a diversity, equity, and inclusion lens, and how does one leverage it when making business decisions? According to Sonali Balajee, Senior Fellow at the Hass Institute, when making a business decision impacting a policy, program, or system, four considerations should be factored into the process.[52] These factors include:

1. People
2. Place
3. Process
4. Power

Let's examine each of these four factors of Balajee's model to gain a better understanding of how to apply a DEI lens to inform your organization's decision making process.

Equity and Empowerment Lens

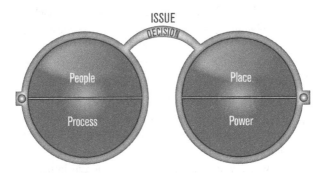

Figure 3.2[53]

1. **People.** As a business owner, I have incorporated this lens into my company's hiring process. For example, when I was searching for a marketing associate, I evaluated how a new employee could potentially impact the people of my firm, and more specifically, I considered who would and would not benefit when it comes to fellow staff, clients, and contractors. I knew I would benefit from having an additional person on my team; however, I also recognized some of my clients who enjoyed having direct access to me may have a different experience.

    When applying this aspect of the model, Balajee encourages leaders to consider the physical, spiritual, emotional, and contextual effects that impact people by asking the following questions:
    - Who is positively and negatively affected (by this issue and how)?
    - How are people differently situated in terms of the barriers they experience?
    - Are people traumatized or retraumatized by your decision area?

2. **Place.** I then examined how a marketing associate would impact the place, or the workplace environment, and other people's sense of safety and feeling valued. Since the marketing associate I hired would work remotely, I knew training and coaching on the front end was essential. Centering initial new employee orientations

around the public values of my firm was paramount, given I'm in the business of role modeling DEI values and everyday practices. Additionally, I committed to provide coaching around sustainable business practices to limit my business' impact on the environment.

When applying this aspect of the model, Balajee encourages leaders to consider what geographic locations are impacted by asking the following questions:

- How are you or your decision area accounting for people's emotional and physical safety, and their need to be productive and feel valued?
- How are you considering environmental impacts as well as environmental justice with respect to your decision area?
- How are public and private resources, including investments, distributed geographically?

3. **Process.** Before moving forward with the marketing associate search, I examined how I would structure the process. How would I prioritize high potential candidates that weren't exactly like me, and what supports could I build within my firm to incentivize them to stay? I wanted to make sure that I was hiring a highly motivated person who wasn't necessarily a white, male, living in the same city as me. I made it a point in the job announcement to prioritize hiring women, people of color, LGBTQ people, people with different abilities, and Veterans. I also wanted to emphasize that I valued working styles and approaches to assignments that offered prospective candidates flexibility and creativity.

When applying this aspect of the model, Balajee encourages leaders to consider the decision making process to resolve an issue by asking the following questions:

- How are we meaningfully including or excluding people (i.e., communities of color, low-income communities, people of faith, etc.) who are affected?
- What policies, processes, and social relationships contribute to the exclusion of communities most affected by inequities?
- Are there empowering processes at every human touchpoint?
- What processes are traumatizing, and how do we improve them?

4. **Power.** The last aspect of informing the job search involved considering the power differentials involved. The central question I considered based off of this lens was how my hiring decision might better include the voices and perspectives of underrepresented people who interface with my business on a daily basis. I wanted prospective candidates to know they would be intentionally encouraged to bring their authentic self to this work. From this examination, I knew that hiring the most qualified candidate, one with different ideas, identities, and working styles from my own, would be most ideal in complimenting my business.

When applying this aspect of the model, Balajee encourages leaders to consider the power differentials involved to resolve an issue by asking the following questions:

- What are the barriers to doing diversity, equity, and inclusion work?
- What are the benefits and burdens that communities experience with this issue?
- Who is accountable?
- What is your decision making structure?
- How is the current issue, policy, or program shifting power dynamics to better integrate voices and priorities of underrepresented communities?

While incorporating this lens may feel like additional work, you and your team will quickly understand how this process helps identify unconscious biases embedded within your current practices as well as understanding where your DEI values live within your daily work. When I incorporated this lens into my firm's hiring process, it took less than 15 minutes to consider answers to some of these questions. At the end of the day, it produced an invaluable hiring and onboarding process that appealed to a diverse pool of talented candidates for a position with my firm. The point of this illustration intends to inspire you to consider how to take this model and infuse it into aspects of your organization's decision making process.

Utilizing your business values and your DEI lens as a guide to informing your daily business decisions will help you implement your organization's values into everyday practice, and leads to more stakeholders feeling like they belong. The next section of the book helps you articulate the business case for why cultivating a workplace culture of belonging helps improve your bottom line. It also underscores the human imperative of this work. You will walk away with greater confidence when you have to make a business case to your colleagues.

CHAPTER 3 - BELONGING BASICS

- The workplace has the potential to disrupt the loneliness epidemic.
- Cultivating a feeling of belonging at work is often overlooked by business leaders.
- Implicit culture contributes to employees feeling like they don't fit in at work.
- Aligning your DEI values with your organization's mission helps foster belonging.
- Using a DEI lens to inform your decision making process will help identify unconscious biases.

EXERCISE 3:
APPLY A DEI LENS WHEN MAKING DECISIONS

Directions: For leaders, and those on their way to joining us, we make hundreds of decisions each week. Yet, how often do we pause and take the time needed to consider how our diversity, equity, and inclusion values align with our decisions? This exercise is designed to help you consider how to take this additional step.

1. Identify a business decision you recently made

   • Describe the business decision you made.

   _____

   _____

   _____

   _____

   • Identify 3 factors that informed this decision. Did your workplace's diversity, equity, and inclusion values factor into making this decision?

   _____

   _____

   _____

   _____

2. Identify your organization's publicly stated values.

   • Does your organization already have publicly stated values? If so, please state them below, and if not, develop 3–4 values that you believe your business centers its everyday practices around (i.e., cooperation, respect, excellence, etc.).

   _____

   _____

_____

_____

- If your organization does not have publicly stated values, list the person or group of people you would need to approach to develop them, and consider how you would make the case to develop them.

_____

_____

_____

_____

5. Utilize the four factors (people, place, process, and power) of the DEI lens and the associated questions featured in this chapter.

- List at least one question from each of the four factors that would have helped inform the decision you recently made below:

  People: _____

  Place: _____

  Process: _____

  Power: _____

- Review your answer to each question above, and describe below if you would make a different decision based on your responses.

_____

_____

_____

_____

_____ **THOUGHT LEADER LESSONS** _____

Why do you think the conversation of belonging at work is gaining so much momentum in the diversity, equity, and inclusion field?

66 Belonging is a basic human element. When we came out with our equity and empowerment lens, one of the quadrants that we used around the relational worldview is this concept of spirit. We included it to give breadth, to give meaning, to give value, which is such a clear human element. In some ways, I would argue that employees are seeking out meaning, purpose, connection, and belonging as an alternative to the devaluing of human life that is happening in our national conversation. 99

– Ben Duncan, Chief Diversity and Equity Officer,
Multnomah County Office of Diversity and Equity

66 Belonging is the result of how it intrinsically feels to know that an organization values my diversity, and has made sure that my voice is included. It's the embodiment of how it feels to work in a diverse and inclusive organization. 99

– Jennifer Brown, President & CEO, Jennifer Brown Consulting

66 The idea of belonging makes everybody feel welcome, where everyone has an opportunity. It helps shift the culture in the workplace to one where the team is working towards the 'we all belong' theory. It gives us a better sense of what success looks like – when people know they belong. 99

– Kylar Broadus, Global Human Rights Activist,
Lawyer, Business Law Professor

❝ Given the fact that we work long hours, Americans are pretty overworked, I think we should want to belong to our respective workforces, we should want to belong to the community at our employer. We should want to feel like we belong because in some respects we're spending more if not relatively equal time with other people than our families. So it's important to create that sense of belonging, and it's important to build that sense of community, and to feel like you're contributing to something. ❞

– Joel Brown, Chief Visionary Officer, Pneumos

PART II

WHY BELONGING AT WORK MATTERS

THE FUTURE OF WORK HAS ARRIVED

❝ Diversity in the world is a basic characteristic of human society, and also the key condition for a lively and dynamic world as we see today. ❞
– Jintao Hu

THE DIGITAL REVOLUTION

In 1947, Bell Laboratories introduced the world to the **Digital Revolution** with the invention of the transistor. Transistors are the basic building blocks of modern electronic devices starting with the transistor radio and moving to devices like the personal computer, the internet, and a plethora of other digital technologies. With the transistor, the workplace as we knew it radically transformed, and so too the world. These digital technologies have connected us in unprecedented ways, making our labor market one that is irreversibly global.

According to the Society for Human Resources Management, a snapshot of today's global workforce includes the following traits:

- An older, more gender and ethnically diverse workforce, with increased interconnectivity.
- Country of origin and ethnicity no longer dictate a worker's geographical scope, especially with developing countries.
- Working from remote locations no longer prevents employees from communicating with their colleagues, allowing teams to collaborate with ease across national borders and time zones.

- Increased global connectivity means that workers can move around more frequently and might choose to migrate for both permanent and temporary jobs.[54]

Global shifts in the marketplace also impact local and regional labor markets. In the United States for example, people of color will make up more than 50 percent of the U.S. population by 2045, and there will be no single racial majority demographic in the country.[55] Given these changes, coupled with the impact of the Digital Revolution on the global workforce, let's consider how these forces impact our sense of belonging at work, and our ability to adapt to ensure our organizations thrive into the future.

Today, we have an enormous opportunity due to the labor market disruptions caused by the Digital Revolution. We now have access to digital technologies helping us more fully engage our people and our customers because of the Digital Revolution. These technologies enhance our ability to cultivate a sense of belonging at work. To successfully adapt to the changing landscape, let's examine how workplaces survived the Industrial Revolution to inform where we are now and where can go. Examining the past may offer some helpful guidance that can empower us with the confidence we need to respond and adapt to the changing trends in the global workforce.

HISTORICAL WORKFORCE SHIFTS

The Industrial Revolution transformed the means of production with the simple, yet genius, invention of the interchangeable part. Instead of producing goods like clothing or cooking utensils by hand, interchangeable parts made it possible to produce these same products with machines. Ultimately, this discovery led to the creation of new products like the steam engine, which powered the rise of mass production and factory jobs. The Industrial Revolution resulted in a "new normal," with an unprecedented rise in global wealth for the dominant class, more jobs for the working class, and an increased awareness of class consciousness with the development of the Labor Movement.

With respect to the workplace, the Industrial Revolution disrupted how the economy and labor was organized. With the high demand for factory labor, the working class went from 25% of the working population to nearly 60% by the end of the nineteenth century.[57] Yet, as the Industrial Age found its stride, the standard of living for the working class did not

Historical Workplace Revolutions

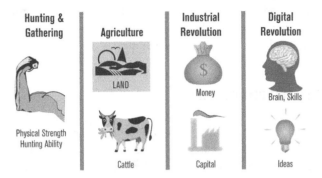

Figure 4.1[56]

improve, and many experienced less freedom working much longer hours, sometimes up to 16 hours a day, compared to their former roles as serfs.[58]

As a result, factory workers were alienated from their jobs and felt a sense of isolation in their workplaces. Rather than having the opportunity to create and complete a project from start-to-finish, factory workers were resigned to contribute some small function of the means of production. At the end of each day, they rarely, if ever, could take credit for the completion of a factory product. Many factory workers were viewed as "interchangeable," as their repetitive roles required a low level of skill, rendering the sense of belonging at work an almost impossible feeling.

THE 21ST CENTURY WORKFORCE

Similar to the Industrial Revolution, the Digital Revolution is bringing greater numbers of workers together. The rise in global trade and the expansion of multinational corporations have increased the level of *cross-cultural collaboration*. This kind of collaboration often bridges cultural and geographic differences. As the Industrial Revolution concentrated the working class into factories situated in urban areas, the Digital Revolution has opened access to a world-wide talent pool, ultimately creating a more global workforce, and this trend will only continue into the future.[59]

As more workplaces open up their doors to the global talent pool, they must understand some of the demographic shifts at hand. The global workforce is aging and becoming more ethnically and gender diverse.

At the same time, as they compete for the best and brightest talent, they must remember that culture goes far beyond simply thinking about age, gender, race, and ethnicity. In order to create a sense of belonging for all, workplaces must consider the cultural diversity of people with different backgrounds, ideas, experiences, and abilities.

MANAGING CULTURAL DISTANCE

When it comes to cultivating a culture of belonging, organizations may struggle to balance their company's values with the cultural norms and expectations of their global workforce. For example, the Ugandan government passed a bill in 2014 making it punishable by life in prison to simply to be a LGBTQ person.[60] An online petition urged multinational corporations in the country to leverage their clout and pressure the government to rescind this law. Citibank and Barclays, two of Uganda's biggest banks were encouraged by advocates to take a public position condemning this law.[61]

Leading up to the law's passage, Barclays issued the following statement:

> *Barclays has a strong history of supporting all aspects of diversity, both in the workplace and in wider society. Equally, we are proud of playing our part in the development of economies across Africa, and the key role Barclays plays in the lives of millions of our African customers. Barclays is aware of the proposed legislation [impacting LGBTQ people] in Uganda and we are engaging at appropriate levels of the Ugandan Government to express our views.[62]*

Citibank followed with this statement:

> *While the laws and cultural norms in some countries where Citi operates differ from commonly accepted global standards for human rights, Citi supports equality without regard for, among other personal characteristics, race, gender, gender identity or expression, disability, age, nationality, or sexual orientation.*

Both banks demonstrate one approach to manage the cultural distance, or the gap between their organizations' values and the laws of Uganda.

This distance demonstrates the friction around a workplace's commitment to LGBTQ diversity, equity, and inclusion, and the challenges of operating in a part of the world where the government promotes laws that run afoul to such commitments. In this instance, both banks made strategic decisions to continue business operations as usual, overlooking their values, making it difficult for their LGBTQ employees to truly have a sense of belonging, especially for those living in Uganda.[63]

As a growing number of businesses operate beyond the borders of their home countries, they take on increased levels of operational risk. In the case of Barclays and Citibank, the *potential* risk came in the form of disrupting valuable government and business relationships that contribute to their profit margins. Their commitment to corporate social responsibility (CSR) in this instance has yet to become an important cornerstone to their global business strategy. When successfully implemented, CSR strategies decrease risk and increase opportunities, which can help contribute to a sustainable global community, while increasing an organization's profit margins.

BELONGING ON MULTICULTURAL TEAMS

The increasingly global workforce also introduces challenges related to managing teams and developing employees. Understandably, employees from different cultures and experiences find inspiration and motivation from different sources and incentives. People from different cultures will also respond to a dominant workplace's management and communications styles in vastly different ways. Because cultural diversity contributes to a workplace's overall success, as we will explore in greater detail in Chapter 5, it's essential for your organization to learn how to manage a globally diverse workplace using the latest strategies and skills.

According to Erin Meyer, author of *The Culture Map: Breaking Through the Invisible Boundaries of Global Business*:

> *In the age of globalization, acknowledging — and understanding cultural differences is more important than ever. This is particularly true for leaders, as they have always needed to understand human nature and personality differences — that's nothing new. What's new is the requirement for twenty-first century leaders to be prepared to understand a wider, richer array of work styles than ever before and to be able to*

determine what aspects of an interaction are simply a result of personality and which are a result of differences in cultural perspective.[64]

Our global workforce contributes to creativity, innovation, and new ways of thinking influenced by different cultural beliefs, backgrounds, and experiences. Workplaces that value the strengths rooted within these differences, and understand how to leverage them to attract new talent and appeal to the global workforce, will remain relevant towards the end of this century.

Education and skill levels are a key differentiator between the Digital and Industrial Revolutions. Today's workforce consists of people with better education and more skills, as compared to the low-skilled workers who migrated to factories and mills during the height of the Industrial Revolution. The number of educated people between developed and less developed countries is near parity, and more educated workers are migrating abroad in search of better opportunities and wages.[65]

RETHINKING ORGANIZATIONAL STRUCTURES

The Digital Revolution has also radically restructured how we organize our people. Some labor economists estimate that over the next 30 years, workers will be categorized into three core groups: 1) permanent contract employees; 2) independent contractors; and, 3) temporary employees dedicated for seasonal work when demand for products and services is high.[66] The restructuring of the global talent pool will also radically transform how employers approach employee compensation, contracting, insurance, and other employee benefits.

Rather than migrating to another country for better opportunities, many higher skilled workers now have a choice. Some choose to stay in their home countries and pursue remote permanent, contract, or temporary work assignments to meet short-term labor needs. This option increases flexibility for international workers and also offers opportunities for businesses to hire on-demand without having to endure ongoing costs that are associated with permanent employees.

The greatest challenge with this shift in the structure of talent within an organization is the burden it places upon management. Managers responsible for permanent, contract, and temporary employees must now exercise different management skills to foster a sense of belonging. Employee engagement strategies focused on welcoming temporary team members to the organization, communicating with remote workers, and keeping the team focused on shared goals and interdependencies can help managers navigate these challenges.

The Digital Revolution continues to reshape the way we work. Today, more than ever before, we have access to an increasingly diverse and global workforce. With that kind of access comes great responsibility to build bridges across cultural divides and to cultivate a welcoming culture of belonging for all. Our greatest challenges come in dealing with attracting, including, and sustaining multicultural talent, and in maintaining our business values in the face of human rights abuses that conflict with these values.

Given the complexities of operating business enterprises across borders, the next chapter will outline the business case for cultivating workplace cultures of belonging. This chapter will help you shape a powerful and persuasive message for even those most resistant to this work. It will offer some valuable facts and talking points to consider. Ultimately it will help your organization build the strong foundation necessary to then begin testing solutions on how to cultivate a sense of belonging for your team.

CHAPTER 4 – BELONGING BASICS

- ⊙ The workplace is irreversibly global and interconnected.
- ⊙ Shifting demographics and digital technologies offer new opportunities to engage cross-cultural teams.
- ⊙ The Digital Revolution is the "Industrial Revolution" of our lifetime.
- ⊙ The global workforce is aging and becoming more ethnically & gender diverse.
- ⊙ Businesses must balance their values with cultural norms of the countries they operate.
- ⊙ Managing the changing nature of work poses new challenges for aligning an organization's values with new workforce management methods.

EXERCISE 4:
HOW IS YOUR WORKPLACE CHANGING?

Directions: This exercise encourages you to reflect on the many workplace changes that have occurred since you first started your career. Please take a few minutes to consider these changes and how they may impact your sense of belonging at work.

1. Consider your workplace's demographics as you answer the following questions:

   - The global workforce is aging and becoming more ethnically and gender diverse. Do you see this trend reflected in your own workplace? Why or why not?

     _____

     _____

     _____

     _____

   - Is your organization prepared to adapt to the workforce's shifting demographics? Is your organization prepared to onboard employees who are of different ages, races, ethnicities, sexual orientations, gender identities, etc. from those currently on staff? Why or why not?

     _____

     _____

     _____

     _____

2. Estimate your workplace's ratio of permanent, contract, and temporary employees.

   - Permanent _____%
   - Contract _____%

- Temporary _____%
- Of the percent of contract and temporary employees on the job, do you believe they feel a sense of belonging at work? Why or why not?

_____

_____

_____

_____

3. Strategies to manage change.

- Identify one way your workplace has helped foster a sense of belonging for employees from different identity groups, work styles, experiences, or who are not currently permanent staff?

_____

_____

_____

_____

- Identify one recommendation you would make to help better foster a sense of belonging for these employees.

_____

_____

_____

_____

THOUGHT LEADER LESSONS

When you think of the future of work, where does the concept of belonging fit?

66 The younger workforce intuitively understands the value of bringing their full selves to work. The furthest group from understanding the value of belonging is the executive level. To truly help employees feel a sense of belonging, executives must hold themselves accountable in everything that they are doing to value diversity, to authentically speak about inclusion, and to consistently practice those behaviors. 99

– Jennifer Brown, President & CEO, Jennifer Brown Consulting

66 [The future of work] is through healing. I think when we learn to heal our own trauma, and we learn to heal our own sense of disconnect, then I think we can provide space for others. I think for a number of people, the reason why it's hard for them to build inclusion is because they've not created belonging and safety for themselves. And usually that comes about by healing trauma, and when I say trauma I don't mean "big T" trauma because sometimes people think of trauma as you have to have suffered some calamity; rather when you think about [a microaggression] that is also trauma. 99

– Joel Brown, Chief Visionary Officer, Pneumos

66 There has to be that buy-in for belonging to have a future in the workplace. If the leadership in a company really wants the employees to feel a sense of belonging and to buy-in, they better put their money where their mouth is. They need to walk the walk, show up, and actively engage. 99

– Ashley Brundage, Vice President of Diversity & Inclusion, PNC Bank

❝ It's got to be all over your company – from the moment you go looking for employees, that your organization is going to take care of your people in the best way possible, and this is just one of the benefits of working with your team. A clear commitment and proof points that your organization is creating an environment that works for everyone is what continues to set successful businesses apart from the pack. ❞

– Kylar Broadus, Global Human Rights Activist,
Lawyer, Business Law Professor

❝ What I've been trying to do in my work is exploring how to help validate the pain of not being seen and feeling a sense of belonging [of leaders and their staff]. Brene Brown's work has helped with strategies I use to encourage [my clients] to drop some of their armor and be less defensive and more open. ❞

– Dre Domingue, Assistant Dean of Students for
Diversity and Inclusion, Davidson College

❝ [A]t a human level, people understand they need to feel safe. All of the trauma informed practices we develop contribute to creating spaces that are physically, spiritually, and emotionally safe. The concepts are showing up in a variety of workplaces. People need to feel this [level of safety] on the job every single day to maximize their job performance, to reduce their stress and healthcare costs, and to increase an organization's effectiveness. ❞

– Ben Duncan, Chief Diversity and Equity Officer,
Multnomah County Office of Diversity and Equity

MAKING THE BUSINESS CASE
FOR BELONGING AT WORK

> ❝ *A diverse mix of voices leads to better discussions,*
> *decisions, and outcomes for everyone.* ❞
> – Sundar Pichai, CEO of Google[67]

It takes every single person on the job to cultivate a sense of belonging for our colleagues and those we serve. Conversely, it only takes one person to toxify the workplace. When I led New York City's Office of LGBTQ Policy and Practice, this statement became my personal mantra. I was working in a system with over 7,000 administrators and over 30 contracted organizations with staff sizes that either rivaled or dwarfed the size of our agency.

Together we collaborated to deliver *culturally specific care* to LGBTQ children, adolescents, and their families in foster care and juvenile justice settings. It wasn't enough for leaders to embrace an inclusive policy. Rather, we had to ensure that *every* staff member from the Commissioner to the office administrator had the knowledge, skills, and confidence to respectfully serve this vulnerable population. It only took one person to compromise this fragile workplace ecosystem.

Due to workplace interdependencies, and the external impacts of the changing global workforce, we must collectively commit to doing the work required to cultivate a sense of belonging for all. This chapter explores how we can make an effective business case expressing the importance of belonging at work to our peers, our leaders, and those we manage.

The business case centers around why focusing on the feeling of belonging will ensure that your organization's diversity, equity, and inclusion (DEI) ethos moves beyond lip service and becomes embedded into everyday business activities.

To effectively make the business case for belonging, we will break it down by examining three different parts of the workplace ecosystem: 1) our people, 2) the markets we serve, and 3) the suppliers we hire to help us accomplish our workplace mission. After reviewing these aspects of the workplace ecosystem, and some of the compelling data that underscores why we must double down on this work, we will then explore strategies on how to make the most compelling business case. We will consider a number of different audiences and different strategies to persuade them. Finally, we'll apply our learnings through a simple exercise designed to empower you to share this message with those who need to hear it the most within your organization.

BELONGING FOR OUR PEOPLE

According to Pat Wadors, Chief Talent Officer at ServiceNow, DEI commitments "are the key to win[ning] the war for talent, to find and hire a diverse workforce, and to ensure fair practices, but they aren't sufficient."[68] The key to winning the war for the best and brightest talent is to cultivate a workplace culture of belonging. In this spirit, Wadors coined the term DIBS (diversity, inclusion, and belonging), which combines a company's DEI ethos with the power of belonging. She came up with this term after realizing that her workplace's past DEI initiatives captured her intellect, yet they fell short of winning her heart.

Wadors' leadership pushed us to begin the conversation of belonging at work, yet most organizations have not started the dialogue. Part one of this book examined what it means to belong and how our need to belong drives many of us to seek meaningful connections with others. When it comes to the workplace, we know having a sense of belonging can help us overcome feeling isolated. When effectively leveraged the workplace has the power to combat the rising public health epidemic of loneliness. A growing body of research communicates the value proposition of opening up the dialogue of belonging at work.

This dialogue is needed now more than ever before as evidenced by Aaron Hurst's book, *The Purpose Economy*. His research confirms, "28% of

The Purpose Economy

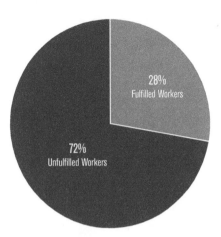

Figure 5.1[69]

the 150 million-member U.S. workforce defines the role of work in their lives primarily as a source of personal fulfillment and a way to help others." While nearly 30% of all U.S. workers feel fulfilled and connected at work, tragically 72% of U.S. based workers do not have a sense of meaning.[70] In order to stay relevant, employers must help cultivate a sense of purpose and belonging for their organizations to thrive into the future.

A wealth of research confirms that **key performance indicators** improve when workplaces invest in proven DEI strategies, systems, and programs. These improvements largely derive from an increase in productivity, innovation, and profit.[71] Understanding why these indicators improve from such investments, and recognizing where belonging fits into the equation, may help us win both the hearts and minds of our colleagues when doing this important work. After all, when employees feel a sense of belonging at work, they become more attached to their organization and their occupation. These attachments are often better motivators than financial compensation for employees to do their best work.[72] But, why?

Having a sense of belonging at work leads to an increase in our **psychological safety**, or a feeling of acceptance and respect, empowering us to be more authentic in our work. As a result, we are more likely to feel engaged with our colleagues, leading to improved employee relationships, team morale, and innovation.[73] The concept of belonging at work taps into

What Younger Talent Wants Should Matter to You

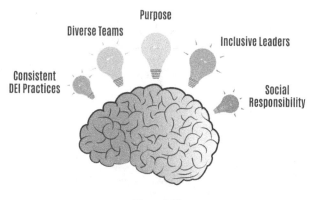

Purpose

Diverse Teams

Inclusive Leaders

Consistent
DEI Practices

Social
Responsibility

Figure 5.2[75]

our primal need to identify with a group, be accepted by its members, and serve as a contributing member to its long-term success.[74] Employers that plan to win the so-called *talent war*, or the competition for recruiting and retaining the best and brightest employees, embrace the importance of belonging at work. Many of these early adopters have already started conversations about what belonging means to their people.

These employers understand that staff engagement predicts their long-term success and relevancy. They spend time trying to understand the expectations of younger generations like *Millennials* and *Digital Natives*, soliciting their ideas about what it means to belong at work, and how to cultivate that feeling in the workplace. They recognize how younger generations hold the secrets to staying ahead of the competition when it comes to competing for the best and brightest. Millennials, in particular, want to join a workplace where they feel they have purpose, and that the organization is helping make the world a better place.[76]

Here's the rub – high potential Millennials carefully assess where they work, and consider several factors as illustrated in Figure 5.2. In particular, Millennials want to *see* diverse representation of people, thoughts, and working styles from the top levels of an organization on down to the front lines.[77] They evaluate how well an organization walks its DEI talk. They also want to help shape the organization, giving them a sense of purpose, and an opportunity to develop professionally. They gravitate toward employers that invest in robust social responsibility programs addressing some of the world's most vexing problems including climate change, human rights abuses, and economic inequality.[78]

BELONGING FOR OUR CUSTOMERS

Cultivating a sense of belonging doesn't stop with our employees. Serving our markets, or our clients and customers, and responding to their needs in a respectful and intentional manner assures an organization's long-term relevancy, helping them thrive into the future. With that in mind, we must work on creating a business case for what it means to not only serve, include, and create fairness for our customers and clients, but to also help them feel that they belong by being connected to the organization's purpose.

For leaders that prefer to see numbers in order to prioritize this aspect of the work, consider a few compelling statistics. When it comes to creating more accessible services and products for people with disabilities, your business gains access to serving more than a billion people, or almost 1 out of every 9 people *on the planet*. People living with disabilities make up the world's largest minority group, and in the United States alone, 54 million people living with a disability surpass the size of people who are Latinx, Black, Asian and Pacific Islander, Generation X, and young people ages 16–24 combined.[79] People living with disabilities also have an annual purchasing power of $200 billion.[80]

When your organization can deliver *culturally specific* products or services, you can help cultivate a sense of belonging and safety for your customers. Culturally specific products or services are those informed by-and-for a target group of people with specific desires or needs. The use of language, cultural norms, and customs familiar to the target group are aspects that inform how to develop these products or services. When your organization successfully meets the specific cultural needs of your markets, your organization ignites consumer loyalty and earns positive visibility.

When a company invests the time and resources needed to deliver culturally specific products and services, the net profit gained from consumer loyalty is significant. For example, when looking at *LGBTQ* consumer loyalty alone, 71% say they would remain loyal to a brand that supports the human rights of LGBTQ people, even if the brand's products or services are more expensive or less convenient to find.[81]

Even though LGBTQ people make up less than 7% of the U.S. adult population, their annual purchasing power is $917 billion.[82] According to Witeck Communications, "contemporary market behaviors are favorably shaped by Millennials who appear to be the most LGBTQ inclusive generation yet." This level of LGBTQ consumer loyalty is amplified by the networks of non-LGBTQ friends, family members, and co-workers who are Millennials.[83]

When it comes to Millennial consumers themselves, they compromise some of the most sophisticated markets, and businesses should take notice as to what matters most to them. Given that they are the largest living generation in the United States, their combined annual purchasing power is $1.3 trillion.[84] Millennials are the most diverse generation in U.S. history[85] and 75% consider a workplace's DEI actions and commitments before engaging with the business.[86] Workplaces that continue to make intentional efforts to cultivate a sense of belonging will get "first dibs" on Millennial consumer loyalty.

Millennial consumers place pressure on businesses to commit to cultivating a sense of belonging and expect accountability for creating a better world in which they belong. Peter Drucker expertly describes the impact of Millennials on how businesses are prioritizing belongingness and social responsibility. In his book, *Managing in a Time of Great Change*, Drucker wrote:

> *Economic performance is not the only responsibility of a business... Furthermore, without responsibility, power always degenerates into non-performance and organizations must perform. So the demand for socially responsible organizations will not go away; rather, it will widen.*[87]

Since the publication of his book, Millennials continue to push organizations to demonstrate their support for economic, environmental, and socially sustainable practices. These business practices make up what's known as the ***triple bottom line***, an accounting term evaluating a workplace's greater business value in relationship to the global marketplace.[88]

BELONGING FOR OUR SUPPLIERS

The triple bottom line extends to how our organizations infuse a sense of belonging to those businesses in our supply chain. Suppliers, or contractors, help our businesses solve some of our greatest challenges. Workplaces that intentionally prioritize procurement spending for socially and economically disadvantaged businesses to serve as contractors help diversify their supply chain, and are more likely to achieve innovation, cost-reduction, and revenue growth objectives. Diversifying the supply chain by specifically working with businesses owned by women, people of color, LGBTQ individuals, Veterans, people with disabilities, and those at the intersections will help improve products and services for those within and beyond your organization.

A growing number of businesses are focusing their attention on including diverse suppliers to participate in their competitive bidding process. Yet, simply including diverse suppliers won't be sufficient in cultivating a sense of belonging for them. Your business should actively outreach the most capable diverse suppliers that align with your organization's strategy and explain how their services can help lead to further innovation of competitive products and services. Explaining how diverse suppliers fit into your organization's broader mission and goals will cultivate a sense of belonging for these suppliers, and inspire them to bid on relevant projects. These outreach efforts are well worth the investment, given that the number of women and minority owned businesses are outpacing the growth of other middle-market companies.[89]

Knowing what we do about the changing demographics in the United States and around the world, committing to diversifying the supply chain will make your business more attractive to the global talent pool, along with new and emerging markets. Your people and your markets will value your workplace's DEI commitments, and you'll be far more effective at communicating them by clarifying how your stakeholders can be engaged with your organization, and feel a sense of belonging. EY offers some guidance on how to unclog your organization's growth pipeline to increase supplier diversity:

Introducing diverse suppliers into the supply chain improves a company's ability to engage with different communities and cultures and also generates a significant return on investment. In our increasingly interconnected global marketplace, every company relies on a network of business relationships in order to succeed. Companies that limit their supply chain flexibility place themselves at risk for poor performance and potential disruptions. Companies with a great number of diverse supply chains that include small businesses often deliver stronger results and are better positioned to respond to rapidly changing market conditions.[90]

The benefits of diversifying your organization's supplier pipeline have the potential to cultivate a greater sense of belonging for your stakeholders. It also has the potential to generate 133% greater return on the cost of procurement operations.[91] In other words, for every $1 million dollars invested in procurement costs, businesses that have a higher adoption rate of supplier diversity programs generate upwards of $2.6 million to their net profit, or their bottom line. Such a significant return on investment suggests that gaining the competitive edge is both the right thing to do, and it makes good business sense.

CHAPTER 5 – BELONGING BASICS

- ◉ Creating a culture of belonging relies on all stakeholders involved at work.
- ◉ Diversity, equity, and inclusion efforts activate our mind, and feeling a sense of belonging opens our hearts.
- ◉ Millennial workers are motivated more by purpose and belonging than by compensation alone.
- ◉ Making our customers feel they belong is rewarded with their consumer loyalty.
- ◉ Welcoming diverse suppliers helps tackle how to create a sense of belonging for our people and customers.

EXERCISE 5:
MAKING THE BUSINESS CASE FOR BELONGING

Directions: Identify the key decision makers in your organization whom you need to make the business case for belonging. Then follow the instructions below and craft a compelling message for each of these leaders.

1. Create a Power Map.

- Obtain your employer's organizational chart, and rank each leader listed on the chart as either a champion (C) or a resister (R) to cultivating a sense of belonging for your people. If you are unsure, you can list them as those within the moveable middle (MM). This group may include people that have the potential to serve as champions with some education and coaching.

   (C): _____

   (MM): _____

   (R): _____

   _____

- Based on your assessment, determine the top 3–4 leaders you must target on the chart keeping in mind their decision making authority to approve, endorse, or influence investing in cultivating a culture of belonging.

   #1: _____

   #2: _____

   #3: _____

   #4: _____

2. Cultivate Your Champions.

- Customize a statement that will capture the attention of the champions on your leadership team. The statement should inspire them to serve as "belonging" ambassadors for other stakeholders at work.

_____

_____

_____

_____

- Share a brief story relevant to this conversation that will support your opening statement, and encourage these champions to endorse your vision for belonging at work. Feature statistics highlighted in this chapter for those leaders who are moved by existing research. Consider internal or external factors that may be relevant.

_____

_____

_____

_____

- What is your call to action for the champions in your organization? Why?

_____

_____

_____

_____

3. Move the Middle.

- Customize a statement that will build interest and compel the moveable middle on your leadership team to support investing in cultivating a culture of belonging.

  _____

  _____

  _____

  _____

- Share a brief story relevant to this conversation that will support your opening statement and build upon the moveable middle's empathy and understanding. Feature statistics highlighted in this chapter for those leaders who are moved by existing research. Consider internal or external factors that may be relevant.

  _____

  _____

  _____

  _____

- What is your call to action for the moveable middle in your organization? Why?

  _____

  _____

  _____

  _____

4. Address the Resisters.

- Customize a statement that will make the case as to why cultivating a culture of belonging matters for the future of your organization, keeping in mind this statement will be shared with the most skeptical.

_____

_____

_____

_____

- Share a brief story relevant to this conversation that will support your opening statement, and acknowledge and address the resisters' concerns and fears. Feature statistics highlighted in this chapter for those leaders who are moved by existing research. Consider internal or external factors that may be relevant.

_____

_____

_____

_____

- What is your call to action for the resisters in your organization? Why?

_____

_____

_____

_____

THOUGHT LEADER LESSONS

What is needed for executives to recognize belonging at work is an essential ingredient to remain relevant?

❝ I talk to clients who say, 'We want to be cutting-edge, we want to be the best that we can be.' Well, to do that you have to be inclusive for the simple fact that if you really want to fulfill the organizational objective, if you want to take care of the planet, you have to leverage the cultural expertise that is around you. You can't do that if you're not being inclusive, because the woman, the gay person, the Latinx person, or the person who speaks a different language might be the key to unlocking whatever solution, whatever potential exists. So you have to take this step if you're really serious about being a relevant and innovative business. ❞

– Joel Brown, Chief Visionary Officer, Pneumos

❝ We need more innovative CEOs who recognize that their most valuable assets are their people. As businesses continue to automate all aspects of the business process with technology, leaders cannot leave their people behind. ❞

– Kylar Broadus, Global Human Rights Activist,
Lawyer, Business Law Professor

❝ Our greatest risk is that we have so much pressure to get work done that we forget how important it is to feel that space and connection with each other. [Leaders must remember] people need to feel a sense of purpose at their workplace every single day. ❞

– Ben Duncan, Chief Diversity and Equity Officer,
Multnomah County Office of Diversity and Equity

❝ I encourage leaders to be more patient and more open to starting a dialogue with their people about what it means to belong. With commitment and more patience, they are more likely to be successful. ❞

– Dre Domingue, Assistant Dean of Students for Diversity and Inclusion, Davidson College

❝ Leaders need a brand around inclusion that is believable, that is authentic, that is backed up by what they do from a diversity standpoint. But how does it look, and how does it sound? How do we see it in action? That's what I want to know as an employee, if I'm looking at my leader. I can tell you the million little things and big things that I hear them communicating or doing through the grapevine or publicly, that convince me that they're a leader who gets it, meaning they're an inclusive leader, or they're somebody who's still struggling to find their place in the discussion. ❞

–Jennifer Brown, President & CEO, Jennifer Brown Consulting

❝ Sometimes you've got to push beyond your fears and say what needs to be said. It might not be the thing that's going to make everybody feel warm and fuzzy, but there has to be some level of accountability for people to actually share their opinion. ❞

–Ashley Brundage, Vice President of Diversity & Inclusion, PNC Bank

UNDERSCORING THE HUMAN IMPERATIVE

> 66 *If you hire people just because they can do a job, they'll work for your money. But if you hire people who believe what you believe, they'll work for you with blood and sweat and tears.* 99
> – Simon Sinek

CLOSING THE PURPOSE GAP

Only "twenty-eight percent of the 150 million-member U.S. workforce defines the role of work in their lives primarily as a source of personal fulfillment and a way to help others," as mentioned in the last chapter.[92] By making marginal gains to give employees a sense of belonging, confidence, and purpose in their work, leading employers will have the competitive advantage of engaging the best and brightest among the 72% – or 108 million – workers in the United States who feel that they lack a sense of purpose when it comes to their job.

Why should we focus our attention on purpose driven workers? After all, isn't it enough to simply ensure our team feels a sense of security within the workplace, remains engaged, and receives fair compensation for their hard work? While these goals help establish a foundation for a healthier workplace, leading organizations gain a competitive advantage when they effectively close the ***purpose gap***. When successful, these organizations attract the remaining 72% of the workforce that feels their contributions lack meaning and importance. They also understand purpose driven workers are the linchpin to cultivating a sense of belonging.

Purpose driven workers exceed key performance outcomes when compared to their disengaged colleagues in the following areas:

- Twenty percent (20%) longer expected tenure.
- Fifty percent (50%) more likely to be in leadership positions.
- Forty-seven percent (47%) more likely to promote their employers, serving as brand ambassadors.
- Sixty-four percent (64%) higher levels of fulfillment in their work.[93]

Given these performance indicators, workplaces successful in attracting and empowering purpose driven talent increase the volume of highly engaged workers who feel a sense of meaning and belonging on the job. These workers align with the organization because they find their work interesting, feel connected to their co-workers, and believe they have a place within the workplace because their work has purpose.[94] Organizations striving to stay ahead of their competitors continue to study what motivates these workers in order to close the purpose gap, or the distance between employees who find fulfillment and meaning in their work, from those who do not.[95]

THE TRIPLE BOTTOM LINE + BELONGING

Employers must close the purpose gap in order to create a sense of belonging for their people. They can close this gap by taking full responsibility for how their daily operations impact their employees, global communities, and the planet. A workplace's commitment to establishing social, economic, and environmental responsible business practices is often referred to as the *triple bottom line*. The Center for Creative Leadership adds additional context for why the triple bottom line matters, especially to workers seeking greater meaning in their work:

> [Organizations] around the world are struggling with a new role, which is to meet the needs of the present generations without compromising the ability of the next generation to meet their own needs. Organizations are being called upon to take responsibility for the ways their operations impact societies and the natural environment. They are being asked to apply sustainability principles to the ways in which they conduct

Triple Bottom Line

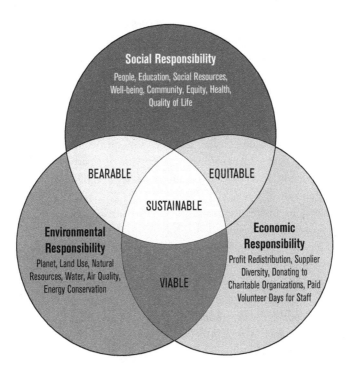

Figure 6.1[96]

their business. Sustainability refers to an organization's activities, typically considered voluntary, that demonstrate the inclusion of social and environmental concerns in business operations and in interactions with stakeholders.[97]

Purpose driven talent gravitates toward organizations with an established triple bottom line.[98] These workplaces communicate their economic, environmental, and social responsibility through their stated mission, values, and most importantly, daily operations. The triple bottom line amplifies a workplace's deeply entrenched values and shares how an organization impacts all of its stakeholders. To get a sense of why this matters in the context to cultivating a sense of belonging at work, let's further explore each aspect of the triple bottom line.

SOCIAL RESPONSIBILITY

Relationships ignite an organization's success, and one way leading organizations are strengthening their connections with key stakeholders is through their commitment to *social responsibility*. A socially responsible organization is one that has prioritized balancing its revenue generating activities with its charitable investments, all while working towards improving the well-being of the organization's stakeholders. Stakeholders may include staff, marketplaces, and communities impacted by the organization's daily operations. When organizations prioritize socially responsible practices, they may benefit from being viewed positively by the public, often leading to a rise in sales, consumer loyalty, and individuals investing in the organization.[99]

What does social responsibility look like from a business owner or executive team's perspective, especially when they are short on time, and focused on improving their shareholders' returns? Richard Branson, one of the world's most successful entrepreneurs, believes that in an era of uncertainty, business communities, "need to work with the social sector to get on top of the problems of the world…small companies need to adopt small, local problems. Big companies need to adopt national problems. Bigger companies to adopt international problems." No longer can business communities operate in a vacuum of unlimited growth and maximum profits.[100]

Branson believes that the future of work, and the future of "doing good" in the world will continue to blend. More purpose driven employees and entrepreneurs will help transform businesses into more socially responsible, "corporate citizens." According to the JUST 100, a listing of the top 100 most ethical and enlightened companies in the United States, "doing the right thing, in every aspect of business, leads not only to success, but fosters excellence and creates industry leaders."[101] The index found that the "most ethical and just" U.S. based companies were also the most profitable and recognized leaders in their industries over the long term.

Simon Sinek, New York Times Best Selling Author of *Start with Why*, says, "people buy *why* you do, not *what* you do. So make sure your purpose is something people can rally behind."[102] Whether you're selling products or services, consider how your business operations impact all of the people involved with the work from employees, to clients, to suppliers, and more. If these stakeholders can connect your business *why* with how it's contributing to making a better world for all involved, you're more likely to attract the attention of those purpose driven workers who value your diversity, equity, and inclusion (DEI) ethos and believe they will have a better chance of feeling a sense of belonging.

If you're seeking ideas on how your organization can invest in socially responsible business practices, consider some of the following ideas:

Social Responsibility Practices

- Dedicate professional development resources to grow and nurture young talent.
- Direct a portion of your business profits to promote local, national, and global charitable organizations to tackle some of the social challenges that align with your workplace's purpose and values.
- Offer paid time off giving staff the opportunity to volunteer for a local cause that aligns with their values and beliefs.
- Offer company matching programs where staff donations to charitable causes are matched by their employer.
- Build community partnerships and engage with local businesses, nonprofits, and government agencies to help tackle social challenges.

ENVIRONMENTAL RESPONSIBILITY

As Millennials attain greater annual purchasing power and assume more significant leadership roles in the global workplace, it is no wonder that they are a driving force compelling many brands to embrace both socially and *environmentally sustainable* business practices. These practices work to balance the demands daily business operations place on the environment to ensure the health and well-being of all people impacted, now and in the future.

When it comes to the marketplace, 73% of Millennials surveyed in a recent study would spend more on a product or service if it comes from a brand committed to environmentally sustainable practices compared to 66% of the total number of people surveyed.[103] Eighty-one percent of

Millennials take it a step further, expecting their favorite brands to publicly declare their sustainability ethos.[104]

Three-quarters, or 76% of Millennial workers factor in an employer's environmental sustainability practices when determining where they will pursue employment.[105] Millennials, more than any other generation, factor these practices into their decision making process, which should make any recruiter want to connect with their leadership team about how to get ahead of this trend. With Millennials about to make up more than 75% of the global workforce by 2030, workplaces must radically reimagine how to infuse a deeper responsibility to their sustainability values to attract the next generation of talent.

As government leaders around the world continue to debate their role to regulate the environment, a growing number of business executives are moving forward as global leaders positively influencing environmental policy. Many of these businesses are embracing some of the following practices. You may wish to infuse these practices into your organization's environmental sustainability commitments:

Environmental Responsibility Practices

- Maintain a paperless office, in which the use of paper is eliminated in daily business operations, and when paper is required, only use recycled products.
- Reuse waste paper (from junk mail), making use of the blank side for notes, etc.
- Recycle as much waste material as possible.
- Recycle equipment that is no longer of use to the firm, including refurbishing and donating items such as computers and printers to public schools.
- Keep energy usage low by using energy saving light bulbs throughout the office and ensuring that computers are shut down after work.
- Purchase office products made with recycled paper like paper towels and printer paper.
- Purchase products with a lower environmental impact like environmentally safe soaps and detergents.

Environmental Responsibility Practices (Continued)

- Use low impact transport for travel to and from work and travel for business. For example: for local travel, encourage those staff who are able bodied to ride their bikes or walk to work, and for others with mobility challenges, consider organizing carpools to and from work.
- Avoid unnecessary travel by making use of instant messaging, video and audio conferencing, telephone, email, and using other technologies.
- Consider the sustainability practices of suppliers before hiring them to ensure that they align with your workplace's sustainability principles.

ECONOMIC RESPONSIBILITY

Larger organizations play a profound role when it comes to expanding economic opportunities for small businesses – especially for those small businesses that have historically experienced barriers to procurement opportunities. Many of these larger organizations have established *supplier diversity* programs. Supplier diversity programs prioritize contracting opportunities for socially and economically disadvantaged businesses and individuals to achieve innovation, cost-reduction, and revenue growth objectives for a business.[106] Supplier diversity programs often encourage businesses owned by women, people of color, LGBTQ individuals, Veterans, people with disabilities, and those at the intersections to participate in competitive bidding opportunities.

When businesses hire diverse suppliers, they infuse a source of innovation and cultural input into the development and delivery of their products and services. When businesses invest in doing the right thing, or expanding economic opportunities for businesses that have traditionally had a hard time getting the opportunity to compete, they also increase their ability to access new and emerging markets. According to the report, *ROI-Related Supplier Diversity* by the Hackett Group Inc., "supplier diversity programs add $3.6 million to the bottom line for every $1 million in procurement operation costs."[107]

If you're seeking ideas on how your organization can invest in economically responsible business practices, consider some of the following ideas:

Economic Responsibility Practices

- Attend a professional supplier diversity conference like the National 8(a) Association Small Business Conference to understand the value of contracting with underrepresented businesses within your supplier pipeline.
- Join local, regional, or national business chambers of commerce dedicated to supporting underrepresented businesses like the National Minority Supplier Development Council, the Women's Business Enterprise National Council, or the National LGBT Chamber of Commerce to name just a few.
- Strengthen your relationships with these business chambers and work in coalition with them to help identify diverse suppliers who have the capabilities to meet your organization's procurement needs.
- Establish a supplier diversity program at your organization and commit to dedicating a specific percentage of contracts for minority owned businesses.
- Establish an annual reporting process to assess how well your supplier diversity efforts are going, and continue to set annual goals to expand economic opportunities for community members impacted by your business.

MASTERING THE TRIPLE BOTTOM LINE

When purpose driven workers consider employment opportunities at your organization, especially those workers who are Millennials or younger, be prepared to talk about specific business practices demonstrating your organization's social, environmental, and economic responsibility. Communicating these practices will amplify how your organization is doing good in the world, and will attract high potential talent who embody the spirit of purpose and belonging at work.

For examples of organizations that have mastered the triple bottom line, consider learning more about some of the 3,000 Certified B Corporations from 150 industries located in 60 countries. These organizations strive to balance their profit and purpose by considering how their decisions impact their people, their communities, and the planet. These organizations have committed to leveraging their businesses as a force for social good. You can find a complete listing of these organizations, and learn more about their journey in building a business with purpose, for purpose driven workers by visiting: https://bcorporation.net/directory.

CHAPTER 6 – BELONGING BASICS

- The majority of the global workforce feels isolated and disconnected from their jobs.
- Purpose driven workers feel a sense of meaning and connection with their colleagues and occupation.
- Purpose driven workers embody the feeling of belonging at work.
- Purpose driven talent gravitates toward employers taking social, environmental, and economic responsibility, or simply, "doing the right thing" in business.
- Doing the right thing requires businesses to allow their values to drive business goals.
- Embracing the triple bottom line will help close the purpose gap, attract purpose driven workers, and cultivate a sense of belonging for all stakeholders.

EXERCISE 6:
WHAT DOES YOUR ORGANIZATION VALUE?

Directions: Consider answering the following questions about what your organization values and the impact it wants to make in the world. Consider some of the factors that may influence how your organization's values align or diverge from the actions it takes to fulfill its goals.

1. Research shows that purpose driven workers value organizations that demonstrate social, environmental, and economic responsible business practices.

    •   Consider your organization's top 3 values, and summarize them below:

    _____

    _____

    _____

    •   Do the values of your workplace demonstrate a commitment to the triple bottom line? If they do not, what would it take to shift these values to communicate this commitment?

    _____

    _____

    _____

    •   Describe how different your workplace would look and feel if employees felt a greater sense of purpose on the job. Do you believe more employees would feel a sense of belonging if they understood how their contributions helped the organization prosper while also giving back to social and environmental causes? Why or why not?

    _____

    _____

    _____

THOUGHT LEADER LESSONS

How does belonging fit into an organization's commitment to economic, environmental, and social responsibility?

❝ I go back to what my grandmother used to say, which is, 'How you do anything is how you do everything.' So it would be really odd to have a sense of belonging internally, but then to have this schism, this disconnect with the people outside the company. If you're there to help people, then I think it makes sense for you to not only create a sense of belonging in terms of the product and the service, but also in terms of how you view them, and in terms of how you connect and how you engage. It shouldn't just be a capitalistic venture. ❞

— Joel Brown, Chief Visionary Officer, Pneumos

❝ The consumer is a little shakier, but the employees are really steadfast, so that's where you really have to invest. That's maybe the less splashy stuff. I think that's the more difficult equation as to really create that sense of belonging in your workforce, because to me that's an investment in the long term. Because those are the people that are touching all of your customers every day. They're the ones that propagate that message. They're the ones that should be steering the social responsibility agenda for the company."

"It should be bubbling up for the workforce. If you get that right, then I feel like the commercial side will flow from it. Then if you're lucky enough to have an activist CEO, who's somebody who just personally is on top of the issues, and doesn't event need people to be telling them what the hot issues are. In a perfect world, every leader would say, "this is my job. I don't even need to be told by the ERG what's going on for the community. I know because of the work I'm doing personally. ❞

— Jennifer Brown, President & CEO, Jennifer Brown Consulting

66 The short answer is yes, belonging fits into an organization's commitment to social responsibility. We have opportunities to share these responsibilities through sharing our stories. 99

– *Ben Duncan, Chief Diversity and Equity Officer,*
Multnomah County Office of Diversity and Equity

PART III

HOW YOU CAN CULTIVATE A SENSE OF BELONGING AT WORK

SERVING AS AN INCLUSIVE LEADER

❝ Tell me and I'll forget. Teach me and I'll remember.
Involve me and I'll learn. ❞
– Ben Franklin

Leaders – and those on their way to joining them – must take an inclusive approach to welcome the new global workforce and attract emerging markets. Changing workplace demographics alone should motivate even the most recalcitrant leaders to reexamine how they show up in the workplace with respect to their leadership approach. Shifting their approach has the potential to more effectively communicate a sense of purpose and belonging for all stakeholders within an organization. To remain relevant, organizations must develop *inclusive* leaders who have the ability to effectively leverage the diversity of people, thoughts, and experiences. By doing so, the organization gains an advantage when it comes to innovating solutions and appealing to changing markets.

Good news! If you've made it this far in the book, you have the commitment, grit, and tenacity required to do this work well, which are some of the traits of an inclusive leader. This chapter offers a framework for understanding what it means to be an inclusive leader, along with what is required to grow into this role. More broadly, this final section of the book offers everyday actions you can take – no matter your role – that will make a world of difference for your organization's stakeholders. These concrete actions will help grow your confidence and knowledge to build a more diverse and inclusive organization.

INCLUSIVE LEADERSHIP

An inclusive leader communicates the feeling of belonging by offering their stakeholders a sense of purpose. They have the ability to connect their organization's mission and values to those they lead, and they ignite a sense of meaning for each and every stakeholder. Organizations led by inclusive leaders will out distance their competition, as they are better positioned to attract purpose driven workers with a strong commitment to the triple bottom line, as demonstrated in Chapter 6. Yet, many leaders struggle with how to cultivate such feelings, and those rising leaders doubt their capabilities when it comes to encouraging their colleagues to voice different perspectives and dissent in a respectful manner.

In order to overcome these fears, worries, and concerns, we must understand what it takes to facilitate the sense of belonging and the feeling of being valued in the workplace. When we reimagine what it means to be a leader, and embrace a new set of attitudes and behaviors, we have the potential to cultivate these feelings. The new model for inclusive leadership moves away from the antiquated paradigm of one leader having all of the answers, to a new approach. Inclusive leaders value the contributions of their stakeholders. They lead from the center, and have the ability to effectively leverage the collective wisdom of the group.

To better understand this new paradigm, researchers have identified six signature traits of inclusive leaders as seen in Figure 7.1.[108]

These leadership traits include:

- Commitment
- Courage
- Cognizance of Bias
- Curiosity
- Cultural Intelligence
- Collaboration

Inclusive leaders embody these six signature traits. They do so by including individuals whose personal values align with the drive to intentionally include the ideas, perspectives, and lived experiences of staff, consumers, and contractors from different backgrounds and identities. They understand and believe in the power of holding space for dissent to help improve the overall business strategy. These individuals have a fierce commitment to inclusion, and have internalized how it will improve their organization. They use their influence to amplify the voices of those on

Inclusive Leadership Traits

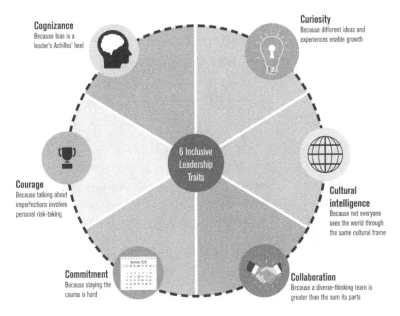

Cognizance
Because bias is a leader's Achilles' heel

Curiosity
Because different ideas and experiences enable growth

Courage
Because talking about imperfections involves personal risk-taking

6 Inclusive Leadership Traits

Cultural intelligence
Because not everyone sees the world through the same cultural frame

Commitment
Because staying the course is hard

Collaboration
Because a diverse-thinking team is greater than the sum its parts

Figure 7.1[109]

their team, sharing the best ideas – giving credit where credit is due – with senior leaders in the organization.

Inclusive leaders understand that change happens when you make people feel differently. In order to elicit new feelings, they know their message must resonate with the mind *and* the heart. In their book, *The Heart of Change*, John Kotter and Dan Cohen introduced the "see-feel-change dynamic."[110] The book's premise suggests that when you show people the compelling reasons for change, you have the ability to elicit new emotions encouraging people to embrace change.[111] While most leaders have the ability to make the intellectual business case for inclusion, inclusive leaders take it one step further and appeal to the heart by sharing what positive changes in the workforce would feel like, introducing new emotions, and inspiring an organization to invest in change.

Inclusive leaders also embrace the value of self-awareness. They understand where their own unconscious biases may show up in their work through continuous self-education and through the feedback of others. To gain this self-awareness, they remain open-minded and curious in order to enhance their ***cultural intelligence***, or their ability to relate and work effectively with others across cultural differences, whether those differences are related to working styles, experiences, identities, or beliefs.

Activate Your Cultural Intelligence

To refine a leader's cultural intelligence, leaders must actively focus on these four elements:[112]

1. *Motivational.* The leader's energy and interest toward learning about, and engaging in, cross-cultural interactions.
2. *Cognitive.* The leader's knowledge of relevant cultural norms, practices, and conventions.
3. *Metacognitive.* The leader's level of conscious cultural awareness during interactions.
4. *Behavioral.* The use of appropriate verbal and nonverbal actions in cross-cultural interactions.[113]

The value of onboarding culturally intelligent leaders in an increasingly global workforce has a tremendous return on investment. When considering how multicultural teams work together, an inclusive leader with a high level of cultural intelligence has the ability to yield positive business outcomes ranging from productive cross-cultural negotiations to improved job performance; especially for teams with remote workers living in different parts of the world.

YOU ARE THE INCLUSIVE LEADER YOU'VE BEEN WAITING FOR

At this point, you may be saying to yourself that you aren't leadership material. You may have convinced yourself that your role doesn't lend enough influence to transform your organization's culture. You may even consider yourself too insignificant to make a difference, and that you don't have the ability to influence your leadership team's hearts and minds to invest in cultivating a culture of belonging. When these thoughts arise, know they are limiting beliefs blocking you from establishing a culture aligned with your values of fairness, purpose, and inclusivity for yourself, with trusted colleagues, or even with your entire department.

Regardless of your role, you too can show your stakeholders what it feels like to belong at work, and inspire them to embrace the necessary culture changes required to cultivate it. Similar to other inclusive leaders, you must first make the commitment to understand your own unconscious biases, and be humble about them. One of the first steps you can take is making the commitment to take a free online implicit association test (IAT).[114] By taking the IAT, you'll have a greater awareness of your thoughts and feelings outside of conscious awareness and gain an understanding of where your hidden biases live. You can take a free test by visiting Project Implicit online: https://implicit.harvard.edu/implicit/.[115]

After you take the IAT, collaborate with your colleagues to identify the cultural norms and values your team celebrates and shares. Take the time to learn about different customs that may conflict with how the team works together, and identify ways to honor different approaches to collaboration. Once you have a sense of your team's values, write them down and share them with prospective employees so that they understand the team's culture from day one. Taking this approach is especially meaningful for staff working remotely or internationally. When values and cultural norms are explicitly stated, members of the team have the opportunity to ask clarifying questions about them, and have a better chance of avoiding embarrassing mistakes or cultural gaffes that could compromise important professional relationships.

For example, Rhiddi was a brilliant computer scientist promoted and relocated from Delhi to San Francisco. Her supervisor expressed concern that she wasn't contributing enough in team meetings. When she shared this feedback, Rhiddi said, "where I'm from, it is considered disrespectful to interrupt colleagues in a public setting." Culturally, she was socialized to wait until other people completed their thoughts before interjecting. Rhiddi's supervisor encouraged her to say, "excuse me," and raise her hand when she wanted to be heard, and she trained the team to give the floor to Rhiddi when she took these actions. These strategies helped Rhiddi adapt to the team's culture without changing her deeply held beliefs about respecting her colleagues.

THE IMPORTANCE OF INTERVENING

One of the most important ways to move up as an inclusive leader is by intervening when you witness *microaggressions* or *discriminatory* behaviors. You can open up the conversation by stating that the behavior you observed runs counter to the organization's commitment to inclusion, respect, and belonging. For example, your boss may have unconsciously planned a workplace event on Ros Hashanah, an important Jewish New Year festival, and expects everyone on the team to attend, "no excuses." A gentle reminder about the organization's respect of diverse faith traditions can help him recognize that several team members observe the holiday and that the date should be moved back a week to make accommodations. This action communicates a sense of belonging, and signals to all your colleagues that their faith traditions, or lack thereof, are respected and affirmed.

You can also serve as an inclusive leader by recognizing where you hold privileges in the workplace, and where you do not. We can best understand these privileges when we consider how our race, gender identity or expression, sexual orientation, immigration status, ability, and religious practices, among other aspects of our identity, offer different levels of privilege and access. Inclusive leaders recognize that their employees may approach workplace scenarios differently due to the privileges that they may or may not hold within the workplace. To serve as an inclusive leader, remember the concept of the platinum rule and work to treat each employee in a manner in which they want to be treated by working to support their specific needs.

For example, a conversation about family life between a visiting supplier and your team may inadvertently elicit a microaggression as the visiting supplier asks your CEO about his wife's cooking. Without hesitation, you chime in that your CEO's husband makes the best vegan beet burgers. Alternatively, when planning travel for an upcoming trip, your colleague, Karen, decides to take an earlier flight, even though she will miss part of the team's weekly meeting. When you ask her why she made that decision, she expresses to you that she doesn't like to travel late due to safety concerns. She shared that when she has taken later flights, she often experiences verbal harassment from men in the parking garage. By staying observant and meeting the specific needs of your employees, you are cultivating a culture of belonging.

EQUITY LEADERSHIP PRACTICES

The final way you can serve as an inclusive leader, no matter your position, is by studying and understanding the difference between equity and equality. As outlined in chapter one, equity recognizes that while we should all have access to fair treatment on the team, because we are not the same, we will need different things to advance within the organization. When you notice structural differences that make it difficult for different members of the team to advance at work, you can shine a light on them without making team members feel tokenized or singled out.

For example, consider members on your team who are parents. These colleagues offer valuable perspectives, as they can help the organization better serve customers raising families. While you want to hold parents to the same performance standards as the rest of the team, you also want to allow colleagues with children to have the flexibility to leave work early to pick up their children from school, or to allow those actively planning families to take the necessary family leave to welcome a new child into the home without penalty. Making these accommodations creates equity by removing the structural barriers that once forced parents to make the difficult choice between their economic livelihood and the well-being of their families.

When embracing the traits of an inclusive leader, no matter your position, you have the ability to elicit a sense of belonging and purpose. Understanding the traits of what it takes to be an inclusive leader will enable you to begin developing new capabilities. As you practice these new capabilities, your confidence will grow. As your confidence grows, you will be poised to apply the five key actions outlined in Chapter 8. These actions will help foster a feeling of belongingness for your stakeholders, as you will gain the skills to help them connect how their work matters and fulfill the broader mission of the organization.

CHAPTER 7 – BELONGING BASICS

- ◉ Leaders must take an inclusive approach to welcome the global workforce.
- ◉ Inclusive leader traits include commitment, courage, cognizance of bias, curiosity, cultural intelligence, and collaboration.
- ◉ Investing in culturally intelligent leaders yields a high return on investment for global organizations.
- ◉ You can move up and serve as an inclusive leader, regardless of your role.
- ◉ Commit to understanding your unconscious biases, identify unwritten cultural norms, intervene when you notice microaggressions, and introduce equitable business practices.

EXERCISE 7:
FLEX YOUR INCLUSIVE LEADERSHIP MUSCLES

Directions: Take some time to consider the questions below and flex your inclusive leadership muscles now that you know what it means to lead from the center. Before getting started, first take one of the Implicit Association Tests (IAT) here: https://implicit.harvard.edu/implicit/.

1. Consider your Implicit Association Test (IAT) results, and list your known implicit biases below. If you have not yet taken the IAT, consider past feedback you received from a supervisor, colleague, or customer who may have noticed a bias you were not aware of.

   _____

   _____

   _____

   _____

   • Next to each bias listed above, identify one action you will take to prevent these biases from adversely impacting future decision making.

2. List the unwritten cultural norms within your organization below (i.e., it's okay to interrupt others during a strategy session, or even though our day starts at 9 am, our boss expects us to be at the office by 8:45 am).

   _____

   _____

   _____

   _____

3. What would it take to encourage your leadership team to enshrine these cultural norms into writing to set new employees up for success? What does it cost new employees if these unwritten norms remain elusive?

   _____

   _____

_____

_____

4. Does your workplace offer guidance on how to intervene when another colleague or stakeholder is disrespected or encounters discriminatory behavior? If known, write this guidance below. If your workplace lacks such guidance, describe how you would intervene as an inclusive leader.

_____

_____

_____

_____

5. If your workplace lacks such guidance, what would it take to implement the approach you described above? What would prevent your organization from investing the time and resources to educate other staff about how to positively intervene?

_____

_____

_____

_____

6. In your own words, what does it mean to build equity within the workplace where different stakeholders are given different supports to fairly access workplace opportunities?

_____

_____

_____

_____

THOUGHT LEADER LESSONS

What are ways inclusive leaders facilitate a sense of belonging?

66 [Inclusive leaders] work to build a relationship, and that doesn't mean you're trying to be somebody's best friend, it just means that you engage someone at the heart level. You engage someone as a human being.

"They model the behavior, so that means that not only do they use the terms of belonging and inclusion, they look for active ways to do that. They're humble, they solicit feedback and input.

"They're not trying to be omnipotent, they're not trying to be know-it-alls, they just realize, hey, if I just ask a question, if I create this space by virtue of the relationship for someone to share with me what their truth is and what their experience is, that goes a long way to creating belonging. 99

— Joel Brown, Chief Visionary Officer, Pneumos

66 It's critical for leaders to have their own personal narrative... a story around when they have felt a deep sense of belonging, [and another story] when they may have felt othered. Stories are a way to draw people in, to create connection between folks, and to compel other folks to reflect on their own experiences... brutal honesty, transparency, self-reflection, and humility are all those things that come with being able to create vulnerability and connections. 99

— Ben Duncan, Chief Diversity and Equity Officer,
Multnomah County Office of Diversity and Equity

66 Embrace the platinum rule by treating other people as they want to be treated with respect, and really get to know all of the experiences of those surrounding you. Take the time to make

real authentic connections, and you'll build a great foundation for helping others feel purpose in their work, and a sense of belonging to the team. 〞

– Kylar Broadus, Global Human Rights Activist,
Lawyer, Business Law Professor

❝ It comes down to understanding that person across from you, and if you don't understand them, then you'd better go over there, speak to them, and find out more about them. Be a better listener and then ask relevant questions that are going to get you to making a connection. That's what I do on a day-to-day basis whenever I'm at an event or I'm somewhere, it's how are we connecting with that other person? 〞

– Ashley Brundage, Vice President of
Diversity & Inclusion, PNC Bank

❝ Never try to do it yourself and be really vulnerable and say, 'yeah I don't know this so let me figure out who I can ask to get it.' Part of that is asking the people in your particular organization what they are thinking the best way to go about [facilitating a sense of belonging] looks like. 〞

– Dre Domingue, Assistant Dean of Students for
Diversity and Inclusion, Davidson College

❝ [Belonging] is a universal and human thing. It's going to be defined in unexpected ways. So somehow we need to really look for the answers amongst groups that have been underrepresented from a demographic perspective, I think we need to ask these questions across the board, as well. Now, more than ever, we've got to assume everybody to some degree is experiencing inclusion and exclusion dynamics. 〞

– Jennifer Brown, President & CEO, Jennifer Brown Consulting

EVERYDAY ACTIONS YOU CAN TAKE, NO MATTER YOUR ROLE

❝ There is only one way to look at things until someone shows us how to look at them with different eyes. ❞
– Pablo Picasso

When I present to groups about building diverse, equitable, and inclusive organizations, one of the most popular questions I field is from leaders concerned with *how* they can foster the feeling of belonging. Many who ask this question share their struggles with where to start, who to talk to, or how to take concrete actions to generate an authentic feeling sensed by all workers, especially those who are underrepresented in the workplace – whether that be because of their identities, working styles, experiences, or geographic location.

This chapter is designed to help you consider the everyday actions you can take at work. It will help you determine what's possible given your role within an organization, commit to several actions you can take in the short- and long-term, and measure your progress over time. While these actions may seem simple, some require a bit more time than others. I can assure you that for the many clients I have helped, these actions truly make a world of difference in fostering a sense of belonging for your people.

This chapter offers five major actions you can take. Next to each of these actions, you'll find a brief explanation of what they look like in the workplace, best practices to consider before you act, practices to avoid, and a short explanation as to why each action is important. The five actions include:

---

5 Actions to Build an Inclusive Organization

1. Commit to continuous self-education
2. Apply an inclusion lens in your everyday work
3. Communicate the diversity, equity, and inclusion (DEI) business case
4. Get involved with workplace DEI efforts
5. Take a leadership role[116]

The exercise at the end of this chapter encourages you to commit to the actions you feel ready to take today. It will help you identify a colleague to hold you accountable and learn to measure your progress over time. As you review each of the five main actions listed below, recognize that they get progressively more challenging as you advance deeper into this chapter. If you are struggling with where to begin, start by diving deeper into the first action. Remember the long-game and begin identifying an action that is both aggressive and realistic.

EVERYDAY ACTIONS YOU CAN TAKE, NO MATTER YOUR ROLE

1. Commit to Continuous Self-Education

Cultivating a workplace culture of belonging is a journey, not a destination. It takes patience, perseverance, tenacity, and grit. The journey starts with yourself by committing to continuous education. Remember that even the most seasoned diversity, equity, and inclusion (DEI) practitioners continuously recommit to this first action. For example, even with two decades of experience doing this work, I continue to learn every single day from my peers, my clients, and the growing body of literature on the topic. Remember that you *can* do it! The following guidance below can help you get started.

──────────────── Best Practices: ────────────────

• Become familiar with the general diversity, equity, and inclusion terminology detailed in Chapter 1, along with any specific organizational language around how these concepts are valued in your workplace.

- Seek out knowledge on your own to learn about the different identities, cultures, races, religions, working styles, perspectives, backgrounds, and lived experiences represented by stakeholders working within your organization. Consider brushing up on how the global workforce and emerging markets continue to shift as outlined in Chapter 4.

- Familiarize yourself with the challenges that people of color, women, people of different religious traditions, LGBTQ people, people with disabilities, immigrants, and those who served in the military experience in the workplace. Recall how inclusive leaders work to consider these challenges and make accommodations for these stakeholders as outlined in Chapter 7.

- Participate in relevant conferences and continuing education opportunities to learn more about the intersections between DEI and your profession. By learning and integrating this knowledge, you are more likely to appeal to Millennial talent who value working for employers committed to walking their talk when it comes to executing upon their DEI values and commitments.

- Participate in community events organized by groups from different cultural backgrounds than your own, and engage with different customs and traditions taking place at these events to experience the world in a new way.

Why It's Important:

By taking the time to self-educate about different groups, experiences, knowledge, perspectives, and working styles within your organization, you are demonstrating a meaningful commitment to this work. You also serve as a *possibility model* for your colleagues who are struggling to get started with understanding why this work is essential. For those paying attention, share your knowledge, encourage them to join you at relevant work conferences on the topic, and share books, such as this one, blog articles, and other relevant information to help educate others.

Practices to Avoid:

- Do not expect colleagues from underrepresented groups to educate you about their customs, traditions, experiences, and backgrounds. You can signal a deep sign of respect to underrepresented groups by committing to your own self-education.

- Do not allow others in the workplace to overlook the importance of understanding DEI nuances in your organization. Connect one-on-one with colleagues who may need some additional support, and suggest that they read some of the materials you found helpful to understanding why DEI is critical to the workplace, and encourage them to also self-educate.

- Refrain from losing patience with colleagues who do not yet appreciate the value of workplace belonging, or who may not always behave respectfully. Often, negative behaviors and biases derive from ignorance or lack of understanding. While ignorance is not an excuse for prejudice, sharing your personal self-education journey may help open your colleagues' hearts and minds.

---

2. Apply an Inclusion Lens in Your Everyday Work

No matter your role at work, there are a number of ways to weave inclusive practices within the fabric of your daily responsibilities. Taking this action will demonstrate your commitment to your colleagues and other stakeholders – especially those from underrepresented groups – that they belong and are valued for their everyday contributions.

Best Practices:

- Embrace the **platinum rule** by treating people in a way in which they wish to be treated rather than the way in which you want to be treated. Common social activities and practices that are comfortable for you may not be comfortable for other stakeholders within the workplace. Self-educate, and build relationships with your colleagues to get a sense as to what would make them feel affirmed and respected.

- Commit to understanding how unconscious bias shows up for you. Consider taking the free implicit association test, and learn more about your unconscious biases. After gaining awareness about these biases, consider ways to get support on how to adopt more inclusive attitudes and behaviors.[117]

- Ensure productive team environments where all members can contribute to innovation and problem solving. For example, everyday actions you can

> Take the implicit association test by visiting: https://implicit.harvard.edu/implicit/education.html.

take include soliciting the opinions of team members who are introverts, making sure that a variety of voices are heard, or ensuring that individuals get credit for their ideas and work.

- Commit to serving as a workplace *sponsor* for underrepresented talent. Remember, sponsoring an employee differs from mentoring an employee. As a sponsor, you must advocate publicly for your *protégés*, ensure that their work is seen in the right places and by the right people, and be willing to spend some of your social and political capital to help advance your protégé.

Why It's Important:

You can work towards applying an inclusion lens in your everyday work by gaining awareness of where your unconscious biases exist. When you are aware of your existing biases, you are better positioned to hold yourself accountable to transforming them into more inclusive attitudes and behaviors. By taking this action, you can successfully foster a sense of belonging for your stakeholders, and your organization.

--- Practices to Avoid: ---

- Do not assume that you are free from *unconscious bias*. According to Renee Navarro, Vice Chancellor of Diversity and Outreach at the University of California, San Francisco, "unconscious biases are social stereotypes about certain groups of people that individuals form outside their own conscious awareness, and *everyone* holds unconscious beliefs about various social and identity groups, and these biases stem from one's tendency to organize social worlds by categorizing."[118]

- Avoid inconsistencies when trying to cultivate a workplace culture of belonging. This means that you must be respectful and affirming for differences in the workplace at all times, and role model appropriately. For example, if you fail to accommodate a colleague who recently suffered a broken leg, and then give a speech to a community group highlighting your organization's inclusion commitment, you have failed to honor your commitment. In this instance, such inconsistencies make it difficult for colleagues with disabilities to feel a sense of belonging.

- Don't isolate your efforts in solely role modeling a respectful culture within the workplace. Remember that diversity of people, opinions, and experiences exists both within the workplace and beyond. As such, consider taking these principles into your communities outside of the workplace, including your home, civic organizations, faith communities, etc.

- Do not fail to intervene when inappropriate behavior shows up in the workplace. For example, if an employee tells an offensive joke that may alienate those who are different from them – even if they are not present at the time – you have the power to intervene and explain why their behavior creates an unwelcoming workplace. Such role modeling will help your colleagues navigate similar scenarios when you aren't around to set the tone.

---

3. Communicate the DEI Business Case

Know the diversity, equity, and inclusion vision of your organization and its connection to the overall business objectives, human imperative, and efforts to foster feelings of belonging. If your organization has not yet developed a DEI vision, or facilitated discussions about why belonging in the workplace matters, identify key decision makers and communicate the business case to them. The relevancy of your organization depends on your efforts to make this business case known to your senior leaders, and to equip them with the confidence to set the tone and serve as ambassadors of this message.

––––––––––––––––––––– Best Practices: –––––––––––––––––––––

- Commit to the process by understanding how diversity, equity, and inclusion impact your role, and how your role impacts the success of building a more inclusive organization where your people feel a sense of belonging.
- Familiarize yourself with the DEI strategic goals your leadership team committed to work towards, and consider how to stitch these goals into your practice. Develop an elevator speech of two to three sentences to describe why these goals matter to your organization.
- Share your message about the DEI business case with fellow colleagues who support these efforts. Practicing with fellow champions will eventually help you engage with colleagues who are less knowledgeable and supportive.
- If your organization has not yet developed a DEI vision statement, or has not effectively communicated this business case to colleagues at all levels, consider identifying key decision makers who can help get the conversation started.
- Provide examples from the media featuring other organizations that have received recognition for their work in advancing their DEI commitments to provide confidence to your leadership team that this work is possible. Examples of organizations that have stumbled in doing this work also offer valuable insights about strategies your leadership team ought to avoid.

Why It's Important:

It's important to become familiar with how your organization's DEI strategic goals tie into your organization's overall mission and how they connect to fostering a sense of belonging. With this knowledge, you'll gain the confidence to respond to fellow colleagues who fail to make these connections, and you'll help persuade them to realize how DEI is great for your people, your business, and the communities you influence.

Practices to Avoid:

- Do not assume that your supervisor has the knowledge or confidence to talk about the organization's DEI strategic goals. Take the initiative to do your own education, and talk with fellow colleagues who are curious to learn more.
- Avoid assumptions about DEI strategic goals not impacting aspects of your practice. Culture impacts every area of an organization, and it takes everyone's effort to create a more inclusive culture.
- Don't spend too much time trying to persuade resisters to embrace your organization's DEI commitments. Part of their resistance comes from fear of change. Spend enough energy to neutralize the fears of resisters with relevant facts about the business case. Remember, even the most recalcitrant colleagues will witness how a more inclusive culture improves the overall performance of your organization once you begin measuring your progress.

---

4. Get Involved with Workplace DEI Efforts

Actively engage in efforts to help your organization work towards its diversity, equity, and inclusion strategic goals. While engagement requires a dedicated amount of time, your commitment represents a valuable opportunity for personal and professional development. When you commit to DEI efforts, encourage your colleagues to join you. When you return from a DEI-related event, plan to share what you have learned, encourage your colleagues to participate in future events, and collectively brainstorm ways your team can apply the knowledge and skills you've gained from these events to your everyday practices.

Best Practices:

- Show up for DEI events and efforts in meaningful ways, such as attending a speaking event about belonging at work. Actively participate by asking questions and engaging in small group discussions.
- Join an *employee resource group (ERG)* at your organization. ERGs are largely voluntary, employee-led groups that can have a few members

or a few thousand. Composition of the groups are typically based upon an aspect of our identity (i.e., race, gender, ability, sexual orientation, veteran status, etc.), or job function (i.e., sales, IT, policy, etc.), and they often welcome allies interested in learning more. ERGS help an organization enhance employee engagement, and improve services and products for new and emerging markets. They empower an organization to access a vast network of diverse talent and suppliers who can help an organization's workforce better reflect the communities they serve.

- Consider chairing or volunteering with your organization's DEI advisory committee, if one exists. By participating on this committee, you have the opportunity to listen and learn from the perspectives of other employees, as well share your own. Also consider volunteering to chair or serve on committees that organize diversity-related events and activities beyond what's available at your organization.

- For organizations without ERGs, DEI advisory councils, or mentorship programs, consider advocating for their development, and work with fellow champions within your organization to establish these programs.

- Consider becoming a *sponsor, protégé*, or part of a *co-mentoring* relationship with colleagues from different identities, backgrounds, or traditions. Serving in one of these roles will allow you to engage in *cross-cultural engagement* with colleagues who are different from yourself. Building cross-cultural relationships will allow you to grow and learn from gaining new perspectives and vice versa. For example, while it might be tempting to serve as a sponsor for a protégé who reminds you of your younger self, you are encouraged to build relationships with people different from yourself in order to see your organization from a fresh perspective.

Why It's Important:

Engaging in your organization's DEI efforts demonstrates your commitment to shifting the culture into one where everyone on the team knows that they belong. It also signals to people from different groups and backgrounds that you care about the success of the organization achieving its DEI strategic goals.

--- Practices to Avoid: ---

- Do not shy away from joining ERG groups where you will be one of the few allies. Your organization's DEI strategic goals are a human issue and a business issue, and requires colleagues from **dominant cultures** to participate. ERGs thrive when allies join and offer support where they can. Simply being in the room offers strength in numbers.

- Before joining a DEI advisory council, first consider if there are limitations to the number of employees joining the council. If so, reflect on whether the council already has a representative with a similar background and experience as your own. If the council lacks such a perspective, throw your hat into the ring and help support the efforts of this group.

- Avoid sponsoring, mentoring, or coaching younger talent that reminds you of yourself. One of the goals of mentorship opportunities is to cultivate cross-culture engagement within your organization. Consider underrepresented groups within your organization and go out of your way to support young talent that has the potential to step into your role in a few years. You will learn much more about yourself and others when you step away from your comfort zone.

5. Take a Leadership Role

Take a leadership role and drive positive DEI workplace changes to create a culture where all stakeholders know that they belong.

--- Best Practices: ---

- Understand the diversity elements you personally bring to the organization. Diversity comes not only in the form of culture, race, sexual orientation, gender, and religion, but also includes elements such as socio-economic background, education level, geographic location, work style, ideology, and lived experiences. Each of us brings to the table a lifetime of lived experiences and wisdom gleaned from those experiences. Our differences add value to the organization and conversations related to our DEI strategic goals *because* of our differences.

- Be a spokesperson for DEI issues that are not necessarily your own. Taking this action may elicit **imposter complex**, or feelings of inadequacy, which persist despite evident success. Since diversity is a human issue, you too have a **diversity story**. Sharing your story as a spokesperson and making the DEI business case to your colleagues will drive positive change.

- Remember that there is strength in numbers, and when you take on a leadership role to support your organization's DEI strategic goals, you are creating a critical mass of groups representing different dimensions of diversity uniting together with the shared goal of creating a culture of belonging.

- If you manage a professional development budget, consider investing in diversity, equity, and inclusion leadership and mentorship programs to help ensure that you and your team are effectively managing DEI culture change efforts in your organization.

Why It's Important:

Each of us has our own diversity story, even those who come from dominant groups represented in the workplace. Our diversity stories connect us to this critical work in deeply personal ways. These stories empower us with the necessary confidence to serve as inclusive leaders. When we clearly communicate our diversity stories, and why they matter in the context to our organizations, we can help inspire our colleagues to join us in cultivating workplaces where everyone knows that they belong.

Practices to Avoid:

- Do not assume that you lack a diversity story. Consider times where you had to veil important aspects of who you are in the workplace, and recall how this form of workplace covering impacted your overall job performance. Your diversity story is your own, and when you share it, you will raise awareness and make important connections to other colleagues who may have felt similarly.

- Do not fall into the false belief that you are not capable of leading DEI workplace interventions. You step into a leadership role every time you share your diversity story with a colleague, and connect it to why it matters for your organization.

- Do not assume that small actions go unnoticed. When you share your diversity story, or center hiring decisions, program budgets, or customer services with DEI considerations in mind, your colleagues will take notice. These small actions provide possibility models for other colleagues to take similar actions, and these everyday efforts make up the fabric to system-wide culture changes.

CHAPTER 8 – BELONGING BASICS

- ◉ Identify actions you can take to cultivate a feeling of belonging at work.
- ◉ Commit to the actions that seem aggressive and realistic for you.
- ◉ Start with actions that center around self-education.
- ◉ Try using a diversity, equity, and inclusion lens in your daily work and decisions.
- ◉ Advance by communicating the business case, and getting involved with diversity, equity, and inclusion efforts.
- ◉ Step up as a leader, share your diversity story, and inspire your team to take action.
- ◉ Remember this work is a journey and not a destination.

EXERCISE 8:
TAKING FOCUSED ACTION

Directions: Now that you have a sense of concrete actions you can take to help elicit a feeling of belonging at work, the following activity will help you FOCUS, or simply **F**inish **O**ne **C**ourse **U**ntil **S**uccessful. After completing this exercise, you will have a charted course to help you cultivate a sense of belonging within your organization.

1. Write a list of the short and long-term actions from this chapter you feel confident in taking over the next year and beyond.

    Short-Term (over the next year): *Ex: Self-educate, join an ERG, learn about organization's DEI vision and values statement*

    _____

    _____

    _____

    Long-Term (beyond one year): *Ex: Sponsor a protégé, join organization's DEI advisory council, work with Chief Diversity Officer to learn how to communicate DEI business case to department managers and supervisors*

    _____

    _____

    _____

2. From the list above, commit to one short-term action you can take today, and break it down into a SMART goal below. SMART stands for: **s**pecific, **m**easurable, **a**chievable, **r**ealistic, and **t**imebound.

    Select one short-term action: *Ex: Self-Educate*

    _____

_____

_____

Specific: Ex: Learn more about unconscious bias

_____

_____

_____

Measurable: Ex: Read 3 books about unconscious bias in the next

3 months

_____

_____

_____

Achievable: Ex: Yes — set one hour aside each morning to read

_____

_____

_____

Realistic: Ex: Yes, though it will be tough waking up an hour ear-

lier each day

_____

_____

_____

Time-bound: Ex: Yes, I will have this accomplished within the

next 3 months

_____

3. Take a similar approach for one long-term action you can commit to, breaking it down into a SMART goal below.

Select one long-term action: *Ex: Sponsor a protégé*

_____

_____

_____

Specific: *Ex: Identify one protégé to sponsor*

_____

_____

_____

Measurable: *Ex: Yes – it will be possible to work with HR to identify a protégé to mentor who is different from myself within the next year.*

_____

_____

_____

Achievable: *Ex: Yes – once a protégé is identified, I will commit one lunch break each month to work on building a strong relationship with my protégé.*

_____

_____

_____

Realistic: Ex: Yes, I understand that I will need to intentionally set aside 12 lunch breaks each year over the course of the next two years and beyond to help develop my protégé.

_____

_____

_____

Time-bound: Ex: Yes, I will have a protégé identified in the first year, and I will continue working with them for at least two years if not longer.

_____

_____

_____

4. Identify one colleague or close friend who would be willing to hold you accountable to your short and long-term actions. Commit to sharing your actions as soon as possible.

    Ex: I have shared these goals with my supervisor as a part of my own professional development, and I have asked them to hold me accountable.

    _____

    _____

    _____

THOUGHT LEADER LESSONS

How can employees, regardless of their roles, foster a sense of belonging?

&& I always believe, like Dr. King said, that everybody's a leader in whatever capacity. And I think there's a difference between being named a leader and actually being a leader. Sometimes, we think, 'well, if I don't have a title, I don't have the power to influence.' And you do. No matter what your role is, if you can show it with grace and with kindness, I think you can influence. I think you can have an impact on your clients, your stakeholders, your peers. Even with your supervisor, or the person who you're managing. 99

— Joel Brown, Chief Visionary Officer, Pneumos

&& I believe that everybody, regardless of position, has power and that they can make change, or we can make change together. I agree that everybody can be a leader regardless of the position they hold. I come from a working class family, and it's how you can manage your manager, no matter what position you're in. You can manage yourself and you can manage the situation you're in. 99

— Kylar Broadus, Global Human Rights Activist, Lawyer, Business Law Professor

&& First and foremost, it is important to help people realize that there are different types of leadership. Positional leaders, are leaders, though their power is actually quite limited. In that regard, because there are so many accountability factors they don't get to have the same freedom that a bridge leader could have. I think having people understand the power of relationship and the power of community and the power of not being tied to those same kinds of rules and restrictions is really a lot of where the agency can show energy. 🙶

> – *Dre Domingue, Assistant Dean of Students for Diversity*
> *and Inclusion, Davidson College*

🙶 You have an obligation to continue learning, no matter your role. Through that learning, your empathy grows, you start to have a deeper curiosity and that curiosity doesn't harm other individuals. You're able to express curiosity in learning in collaboration and partnerships without tokenizing or harming or being inappropriate. 🙷

> – *Ben Duncan, Chief Diversity and Equity Officer,*
> *Multnomah County Office of Diversity and Equity*

FIND YOUR NORTH STAR, SET YOUR COURSE, AND CHANGE THE WORLD

&& *Whatever the mind can conceive and believe, it can achieve.* 55
– Napoleon Hill

ESTABLISH A VISION

When I served as a Senior Advisor for LGBTQ Policy & Practice at New York City's Administration for Children's Services (ACS), I taped this Michelangelo quote above my desk, "I saw the angel in the marble and carved until I set him free." Much like an artist, I had the responsibility of helping others see the same angel in the marble that I recognized. Rather than picking up the chisel, I had to assemble the right City leaders to work together in articulating a shared vision to free our angel, which in this case, was finding a way to deliver more inclusive services for all young people in our care, centering our work around the most vulnerable to mistreatment.

Specifically, I was charged with the responsibility of equipping the nation's largest municipal child welfare agency and its contractors – upwards of 30,000 professionals – with the knowledge, skills, and confidence to respectfully serve LGBTQ children and young people in foster care and juvenile justice settings. For these professionals to understand what was at stake, I had to define our shared vision and empower leaders from across the City to help in communicating this vision. Our vision helped inspire fellow professionals to recognize that our system had the potential of empowering all young people in our care to thrive into healthy and happy adults.

To build momentum and urgency in doing the right thing, I shared the reality that for far too many young people, thriving into healthy and happy adults was riddled with barriers embedded within the very systems intended to help. For LGBTQ young people, the reality of experiencing rejection from family and faith communities, bullying in school, and the likelihood of interfacing with the criminal justice system led many into the child welfare and juvenile justice systems.[119] While estimates indicate that 7%[120] of all young people in the United States identify as LGBTQ, nearly 1 out of every 5 young people in child welfare settings – or 19% – identify as LGBTQ.[121]

While many understood and accepted that there was a disproportionately high number of LGBTQ young people involved in our care, many were resigned to believe that this was just the way the world worked. Far too many lacked the belief that LGBTQ young people could truly thrive into healthy and happy adults. Simply put, the Agency, and the people responsible for sharing an optimistic message with young people, lacked a bold vision. Without a bold vision, the Agency was bound to be stuck in what was already known, and continue treading over the same worn out paths yielding the same dismal results. Sadly, this limited thinking is not uncommon for organizations like ACS. Understanding how it manifests is the first important step to moving beyond it.

FIND YOUR NORTH STAR

Joel Brown, one of the featured thought leaders interviewed for this book, introduced me to the idea of knowing your *anchor story*, or the story of what holds us back. On a macro level, ACS had an anchor story of having exceptionally low standards of what was possible for some of the most vulnerable young people involved with the Agency. Joel also introduced me to the concept of your *North Star* story, or the story that is leading you forward. For those working at ACS, greater awareness and curiosity about why people believed the anchor story was needed before a full commitment to the North Star story could be realized.

The central theme in the ACS anchor story, or what was holding so many professionals within the organization back, was related to the *empathy gap*. An empathy gap exists when one person's unconscious biases inhibit them from truly empathizing with another person who differs from their own identity, background, beliefs, or experiences. The vast majority of professionals working within ACS identified as **straight** and **cisgender**, meaning that they did not identify as a LGBTQ person. Further, many lacked personal connections to LGBTQ people, communities, and cultures, which exacerbated this empathy gap.

The lack of personal connections with LGBTQ people broadly, let alone with LGBTQ people within the organization, made it somewhat easier to debate their existence and question their experiences. In this instance, professionals suffering from the impacts of the empathy gap were more likely to see LGBTQ people as an abstract concept. When a group of people are viewed in the abstract, dehumanizing their existence and experiences can – and often does – occur. When compounding race and class biases, on top of biases towards LGBTQ individuals, the empathy gap widened between LGBTQ young people in care and the professionals hired to meet their specific needs.

Understanding what may hold our organizations back from working towards our shared vision can help us gain greater awareness of what is needed to cut the rope to our anchor story, and begin sailing towards our North Star as illustrated in Figure 9.1. As workplace inclusion champions, one of the best ways we can clarify our North Star story, or our vision, starts by looking within our own hearts. When we remember how basic the need to belong is, and what it takes for us to *feel* that sense of belonging, it will help articulate our North Star and clarify our vision. When we share

Sailing to Your North Star

Figure 9.1

this story, we have the potential to inspire our colleagues, and do the work necessary to begin shifting our organization's culture.

COMMAND-AND-CONTROL APPROACHES LEAD TO FAILURE

Once my colleagues at ACS understood the need to improve services and care for LGBTQ children and young people, many began to embrace the shared vision of improving services for those most vulnerable to mistreatment, harassment, and discrimination. Embracing the vision alone, however, was simply not enough to shift the organization's culture. Vision in isolation is simply a dream. To sail towards the organization's proverbial North Star required significant effort. It required intentional action. It demanded an all hands on deck approach to *do the work.*

A lack of vision, and the absence of a clearly articulated strategy with defined actions to help reach an organization's North Star, sets those leading the charge up for failure. Without these elements, an organization is simply resting their diversity, equity, and inclusion commitments on hope alone to transform the culture into one that fosters a sense of belonging. According to the Harvard Business Review:

> *Firms have long relied on diversity training to reduce bias on the job, hiring tests and performance ratings to limit it in recruitment and promotions, and grievance systems to give employees a way to challenge managers. These tools are designed to preempt lawsuits by policing managers' thoughts and actions. Yet laboratory studies show that this kind of force-feeding can activate bias rather than stamp it out. As social scientists have found, people often rebel against rules to assert their autonomy. Try to coerce me to do X, Y, or Z, and I'll do the opposite just to prove that I'm my own person.[122]*

To avoid the command-and-control approach that forces culture change upon your stakeholders, you can consider alternatives such as incorporating feedback from stakeholders throughout your workplace ecosystem on ideas that can help others feel a sense of belonging at work. Such feedback has the potential to foster cooperation, strengthen team camaraderie, and inform your organization's diversity, equity, and inclusion vision, along with the work required to achieve it.

When I helped ACS establish a shared vision that all leaders across the system informed, something very interesting occurred. The leaders who cooperated and helped shape the vision began viewing themselves as champions for inclusion. They started to own the vision, and they helped communicate why it mattered to thousands of professionals working in the system. When those professionals realized how their attitudes, beliefs, and behaviors were out of alignment with the vision, they were encouraged to act in ways that supported those most vulnerable in the organization's care.

VISION + INTENTIONAL ACTIONS CHANGE THE WORLD

The ingredients to yield a workplace culture of belonging include clearly establishing your North Star, charting your course, and then taking the necessary actions to get there. While your North Star, or vision, and the course you chart, or strategic plan, make up only a small part of the equation, they are essential for informing your actions. Actions lacking vision simply pass the time, and help your executive team "check off the box" to communicate that your organization is doing something, albeit not very effectively. Vision, a charted course, complemented with lots of hard work will help you change the world.

> **North Star + Charted Course + Intentional Action = Belonging at Work**

The efforts you actively make in working towards cultivating a sense of belonging are not static, meaning that you don't create a vision, chart your course, and take a series of tactical actions to cultivate this feeling just once. These efforts are a part of ongoing commitments to help your organization get better and better with time. When we establish our bold vision, we help our organizations constantly strive to be better with time. Our vision, coupled with a charted course, or a strategic plan that allows us to reassess what's working and what's not, will help inform our actions over time.

Reassessing our charted course, much like sailing on the wide open sea, is critical to determine if we are meeting our objectives. For example, if we set out to sail from south Florida to the Bahamas and a hurricane entered our charted course, we would make plans to reroute for our safety and well-being. Similarly, if we are making efforts to help our people belong, and our charted course coupled with the tactical actions we take don't help us reach our North Star, we have the ability to reassess and recalibrate as needed.

Using my time at ACS as an example, we had to recalibrate our charted course in order to help LGBTQ young people thrive into healthy and happy adults. While many professionals were familiar with different *sexual orientations*, or who we are romantically, emotionally, and physically attracted to, many were deeply confused about gender identity, especially with respect to transgender and nonbinary people. To bridge this gap, we recalibrated our charted course by offering professional development opportunities to help staff understand different gender identities, learn why transgender and nonbinary young people are vulnerable in child welfare systems, and gain skills on how to improve their experiences while in care.[123]

CHANGE THE WORKPLACE

If you are uncertain of how to establish your vision, charter your course, or take the tactical actions necessary to help cultivate a sense of belonging, consider leveraging an existing diversity, equity, and inclusion committee or task force. As outlined in chapter 8, if you do not have one already established, consider forming one. These groups are one of the most effective ways to increase engaged stakeholders who champion this work, as well as with others who still need to understand why this matters. According to the *Harvard Business Review*, these groups have a significant return on investment:

> *Task forces are the trifecta of diversity programs. In addition to promoting accountability, they engage members who might have previously been cool to diversity projects and increase contact among the women, minorities, and white men who participate. They pay off, too: On average, companies that put in diversity task forces see a 9% to 30% increase in the representation of white women and of each minority group in management over the next five years.*[124]

New York Times bestselling author, Simon Sinek stated, "vision is a destination – a fixed point to which we focus all efforts. Strategy is a route – an adaptable path to get us where we want to go".[125] As long as you clarify your destination, or end point, even if it feels impossible to reach, you will build a following of passionate champions within your organization who can help foster a sense of collaboration and inform your charted course. Together, you will gain the strength in numbers required to take the tactical and intentional actions required over time. A culture of cooperation helps yield a sense of belonging for all involved.

CHAPTER 9 – BELONGING BASICS

- Clarify what success looks like by establishing a shared vision of what it feels like to belong at work.
- Forcing culture change upon your people in a command-and-control manner results in greater resistance, and will likely increase bias.
- Building consensus around what your vision looks like is a good first step towards building cooperation to improve the culture of your workplace.
- Belonging at Work = North Star + Charted Course + Intentional Action
- Know that having a vision without a charted course is just a dream.

EXERCISE 9:
BELONGING AT WORK INGREDIENTS

Directions: The following exercise will help you apply the belonging at work equation to your organization. Once completed, you will gain confidence in communicating your North Star, or vision, with colleagues. You will also gain strategies on how to inform this vision with other stakeholders, develop a charted course, and define intentional actions you can take today to get started on this important work.

1. **Define your North Star.** Imagine what it would look and feel like to experience a true sense of belonging and purpose at work. How would your colleagues, no matter their position, identities, backgrounds, beliefs, experiences, etc. be encouraged to show up authentically in their work to help the organization achieve its broader strategic goals? Describe what you see, what you hear, and what you feel. Take time with your response, and offer as many details as possible to clarify this vision.

_____

_____

_____

_____

2. **Identify Your Champions.** Identify all of the champions on your team who understand the value of cultivating a sense of belonging at work. For a shortcut, flip to Chapter 5's *Know Your Audience* exercise to quickly list a few of the key stakeholders who can support your vision.

_____

_____

_____

3. **Identify Allied Groups.** Identify all of the existing task forces, committees, employee resource groups, or other groups of colleagues within your organization that are working to meet your organization's diversity, equity, and inclusion commitments. These groups can help inform your vision, and charter your course of action.

_____

_____

_____

_____

4. **Charter Your Course.** Once you have clarified your vision, and identified the champions and groups that can help inform your vision, consider how you would establish a strategic plan to work towards that vision. Is the plan inclusive of short and long-term actions?

_____

_____

_____

_____

5. **Take Intentional Action.** Once you have established a vision and charted a course, reference chapter 8. What actions are required to reach your North Star? Consider building off of the items you've identified in Chapter 8's _Taking Focused Action_ exercise, to inform your plan.

_____

_____

_____

_____

6. **Identify One Action.** Of all the actions you have identified above to reach your North Star, what is one specific action you can take *today* to get started on moving towards it?

_____

_____

_____

_____

THOUGHT LEADER LESSONS

What is your vision for building a workplace where all stakeholders know they belong, are valued, and serve an important purpose?

❝ Leaders who inspire and compel people that the story they build collectively can be better, and bigger, than the story that they hold onto individually helps create a sense of belonging. This builds on a concept I created called the Third Story, or the idea that there's my story, there's your story, but then the third story is the power of creation, innovation, of unlocked potential. The companies who do this well realize your story is valid, and that the other person's story has value, but the synergy that's created by bringing those stories together, and building something better that taps into everybody's potential and genius, those are the companies I think are really doing a wonderful job. ❞

— Joel Brown, Chief Visionary Officer, Pneumos

❝ My hope is that employers figure out how to build that sense of belonging across geographies, across largely virtual workforces. That they really prioritize this, and that people of all kinds want to stay and help build these companies for tomorrow. ❞

— Jennifer Brown, President & CEO, Jennifer Brown Consulting

❝ Remember that this work is not a fleeting moment; rather it's a long-term commitment. It's not limited to when I have coffee with my diversity officer or when I'm away at a conference where I'm around professionals prioritizing inclusion efforts. ❞

— Dre Domingue, Assistant Dean of Students for Diversity and Inclusion, Davidson College

66 At a base level, the motivation ultimately is that we believe that this work actually will improve the workplace. Everybody should feel like they belong, and that they are welcome. To get there, belonging demands that we actively dismantle systems and structures that create harm, rather than remaining complicit with this reality. 99

– Ben Duncan, Chief Diversity and Equity Officer,
Multnomah County Office of Diversity and Equity

66 When it comes to leadership, senior leaders need to be open to the perspectives of other voices within the organization. For example, if a junior staffer wants to present something important about their programs to the senior leadership team, they should be given that opportunity. This type of access creates a sense of symmetry on all levels, and helps foster a sense of inclusion. 99

– Ashley Brundage, Vice President of
Diversity & Inclusion, PNC Bank

66 As long as people are putting their teeth behind the work, it's an important direction to move because [diversity leaders] have never fully described where we are going. We often immerse ourselves in the here-and-now. I do like having a vision that clearly communicates what success looks like, so we have a sense of when we are getting close. It's important to know where we're going. 99

– Kylar Broadus, Global Human Rights Activist,
Lawyer, Business Law Professor

IN CLOSING – BE THE CHANGE!

> 66 *In a gentle way, you can shake the world.* 99
> – Mahatma Gandhi

Congratulations! You've made it to the end of the book. The magic happens now, as you are encouraged to step out of your comfort zone, and do the work. Start by sharing what you have learned with your colleagues. Then apply your knowledge by committing to one action you plan to take. Be sure to identify an action you can take today in order to make your commitment a reality. By doing so, you step into your power as a possibility model for your colleagues and those people and communities your organization impacts.

But please don't stop there. As you know by now, shifting organizational culture is a long-game practice. Thankfully, it is often the little things that can make a world of difference to those who often feel excluded from your organization. Your patience, consistency, and commitment to the work will yield the changes you wish to see over time. The good news – you can lead on this work, no matter your role, as outlined in Chapter 8.

Now that you have gained additional knowledge and skills, I urge you to confidently take the leap and get started. For additional support beyond this book, please visit the *Belonging at Work* website: www.rhodes-perry.com/belongingbook. It offers additional educational resources and support. You can access this content, along with the worksheets featured in this book, with the password: **Belonging2018**. As I continue to gain new insights on this ever evolving concept of belongingness, I will add new resources, recommended readings, and other educational items to the website.

While this book comes to an end, please know your journey has just begun. As with every new beginning, fear, self-doubt, and a healthy dose of the imposter complex can creep in. Know that if you have made it all the way through this book, you have the kind of commitment and perseverance required to lead on this work, no matter your role. Rest assured you have strength in numbers as you travel this path, as I am one of many mentors ready, willing, and excited to work with you as you grow in your role as an inclusive leader.

As you get started, please share your successes, your challenges, and your reflections on this work by connecting with me online. The best place to find me is at:

www.rhodesperry.com

or

www.outentrepreneur.com

Know that I believe in you, and I know you have the power to do this work. The time has come to release your anchor, chart your course, and set sail towards your North Star. I know you can get there, and I'm rowing the boat alongside you. Together, let's cultivate workplace cultures of belonging.

GLOSSARY

The following diversity, equity, and inclusion terms clarify some of the concepts and themes described in this book. Its purpose is to open dialogue around the central ideas featured in the text and establish a framework around what it means to belong at work. For a more complete glossary of terms, please visit: www.rhodesperry.com/belongingbook and use the password: **Belonging2018.**

Achievement Gaps – The achievement gap in educational settings describing the disparity in academic performance between different groups of students.

Anchor Story – The story we tell ourselves that holds us back from achieving our full expression and potential.

Assigned Female at Birth – A sex assignment determined at either the time of an infant's birth or through prenatal sex discernment in which a midwife, nurse, or physician inspects the genitalia of the infant and assigns a sex. An infant assigned female at birth is a person of any age and irrespective of their current gender identity whose sex assignment at birth resulted in a declaration of "female." For example, when a physician announces, "it's a girl!"

Belonging – A sense of fitting in or feeling like you are an important member of a group. When you belong, you are a recognized member of a group. A feeling of *belonging* describes a sense of authentically feeling in solidarity with others especially with family, friends, colleagues, community associations, faith communities, etc.

Champion – A colleague who goes above and beyond to embrace the buy-in, execution, and success of a social cause, strategic goal, policy, program, service, etc. They typically use their clout and influence within an organization to overcome entrenched resistance to change by serving as ambassadors across the organization. Sometimes referred to as change agents, idea champions, change advocates, etc.

Cisgender – An adjective describing a person whose gender identity aligns with the sex they were assigned at birth. *Non-transgender* may be used as a synonym.

Co-Mentorship – A mutual mentorship between two colleagues both committed to facilitating each other's professional development. Different from traditional notions of "mentorship," co-mentorship balances power differentials, meaning that both partners serve as mentors and mentees simultaneously to more fully learn from and support each other.

Cover – An action where an individual intentionally downplays or omits disclosure of a known stigmatized identity to fit in with the dominant culture. For example, an employee may omit that they are planning to adopt a child and become a parent for fear of losing out on a promotion or stretch assignment.

Cross-Cultural Engagement – An experience where one person or group of people have the opportunity to immerse and engage in the cultural traditions of another person or group of people. Cultural traditions may include, but are not limited to, architecture, fine arts, music, artifacts, language, foods, crafts, leisure activities, faith traditions, etc.

Culture – A social system of meaning and custom that is developed by a group of people to assure its adaptation and survival. These groups are distinguished by a set of unspoken rules that shape values, beliefs, habits, patterns of thinking, behaviors and styles of communication.

Cultural Intelligence (CQ) – The ability to relate and work effectively with others across cultural differences, whether those differences are related to working styles, experiences, identities, or beliefs.

Culturally Responsive – The ability to effectively interact and work with people of different cultural identities than your own. This concept differs from "cultural competency" because it focuses on self-responsiveness and empathy rather than striving to achieve a state of expertise on a culture that is not your own.

Culturally Specific – Products or services informed by and for an individual or group with specific needs. The use of language, cultural norms, and customs familiar to the target group help create a sense of belonging and safety, especially when those delivering these products or services are reflective of the communities intended to receive them.

DEI – An acronym that stands for diversity, equity, and inclusion.

Digital Natives – Also known as Generation Z, represents the demographic cohort following the Millennials or Generation Y. A wide variety of competing names are also used when referring to this cohort of people. While demographers typically use the beginning of the twenty-first century as the starting point for this Generation, few agree on the ending birth years.

Digital Revolution – A term referencing the widespread changes brought about by digital computing and communications technology during the latter half of the twentieth century. Similar to the Agricultural Revolution and the Industrial Revolution, the Digital Revolution symbolizes the changes in how society and the workplace are structured with the advent of the Information Age.

Discrimination – Overt, big actions based on prejudice that unfairly treat a person differently because of, or punish them for, an aspect of their identity.

Diversity – An environment where a variety of different individuals, groups, and/or communities with different social and cultural characteristics exist together. Diversity can also reference diversity of experiences or thought, where a group of people thinking independently have the opportunity to work together.

Diversity Story – The concept that every person has a diversity story, and that that story can help build empathy and commonality with other people and communities different from them.

Dominant Culture (or Dominant Groups) – Power and advantages benefiting a dominant identity group derived from the historical oppression and exploitation of other identity groups. A dominant group, for example, is one that is advantaged, and has superior resources and rights in a society.

Empathy – The capacity or ability to understand, be aware, and be sensitive to the feelings, thoughts, and experiences of another person related to either the past or present.

Empathy Gap – Unconscious biases that make it difficult for people to truly empathize with people who are different from their own identities, backgrounds, beliefs, or experiences.

Employee Resource Group – Largely voluntary, employee-led groups that can have a few members or a few thousand. Composition of the groups are typically based upon an aspect of our identity (i.e., race, gender, ability, sexual orientation, veteran status, etc.), or job function (i.e., sales, IT, policy, etc.), and they often welcome allies interested in learning more. ERGS help an organization enhance employee engagement and improve services and products for new and emerging markets. They empower an organization to access a vast network of diverse talent, and suppliers who can help an organization's workforce better reflect the communities they serve.

Environmental Sustainability – A business principle practiced by an organization committed to overcoming the demands daily business operations place on the environment to ensure the health and well-being of all people impacted, now and into the future.

Equality – Evenly distributed access to resources and opportunities necessary for a safe and healthy life; uniform distribution of access to ensure fairness.

Equity – Fair treatment, access, opportunity, and advancement while simultaneously striving to identify and eliminate structural barriers that have prevented the full participation of some groups.

Gender History – Information related to a transgender or non-binary person's sex, name and pronouns assigned at birth, as well as aspects of their past social, legal, and/or medical transition(s).

Gender Identity – A person's internal sense of being male, female, or for some people, a blend of both, neither, or something different.

Golden Rule – Encourages you to treat others the way in which you want to be treated.

Groupthink – The practice of thinking or making decisions as a group in a way that discourages creativity or individual responsibility.

Identity Group – A particular group, culture, or community with which an individual identifies or shares a sense of belonging.

Impact – The effect an action had on a person, group, or community.

Imposter Complex – A feeling of inadequacy or self-doubt that persists despite evident success.

Implicit Culture – A workplace culture that overlooks the importance of aligning and informing an organization's inclusion values, beliefs and behaviors in support of the overall mission or business strategy leading to an unfocused culture/strategy dynamic and poor business results.

Inclusion – Cultivating an environment where any individual or group can be and feel welcomed, respected, supported, and valued to fully participate.

Inclusive Leader – A form of leadership that intentionally welcomes and incorporates the contributions of all stakeholders within an organization to encourage teams to voice different perspectives, discuss dissent, and inform the overall business strategy.

Intention – An action a person, group, or community meant to do.

Intentional Culture – A workplace culture that continuously aligns and informs an organization's inclusion values, beliefs and behaviors in support of the overall mission or business strategy leading to a purposeful and focused culture/strategy dynamic and better business results.

Intersectionality – Having multiple identities that intersect like gender, race, and sexual orientation, which sometimes can offer advantages in some ways, but disadvantages in other ways.

Key Performance Indicators – A quantifiable measure used to evaluate the success of an organization, employee, etc., in meeting objectives for performance. Sometimes referred to as KPIs.

LGBTQ – An acronym used to describe lesbian, gay, bisexual, transgender, and queer people. It also includes those people questioning either their sexual orientation or gender identity. The acronym typically describes any person who does not identify as either straight (heterosexual), and/or cisgender (non-transgender).

Lived Experience – Refers to a person's unique experiences and choices, and the wisdom they have gained from them.

Microaggressions – Brief, everyday exchanges that send denigrating messages to certain individuals because of their group membership.

Millennials – Also known as Generation Y, is the generation following Generation X. Those who are a part of this generation were born in the early 1980s through the mid 1990s. Since this generation lacks precise dates for when it starts or ends, demographers typically define those within this generation as reaching young adulthood in the early twenty-first century.

Minority Stress – Describes the chronically high levels of stress endured by members of underrepresented groups in society, often caused by interpersonal or organizational microaggressions and discrimination.

North Star Story – The story we tell ourselves that leads us towards achieving our full expression and potential.

Oppression – A state of being subject to unjust treatment or control. Oppression can occur at the individual level or systemic level. As an example of individual oppression, a manager can consciously or unconsciously oppress an employee by denying them a promotion due to a physical disability. An example of systematic oppression, an organization refusing to provide workplace accommodations to employees with physical disabilities.

Platinum Rule – Encourages you to treat others in the way that they want to be treated, as opposed to the golden rule of treating others in the way in which you want to be treated.

Possibility Model – A person who reveals one possible way of being human in this world that resonates with another person. The phrase, "you have to see it, to be it," helps one understand the power and importance of possibility models.

Privilege – Power and advantages benefiting a dominant identity group derived from the historical oppression and exploitation of other identity groups.

Protégé – Often a junior employee who is guided and supported by a more seasoned and influential professional serving as a sponsor or mentor of the protégé.

Psychological Safety – A shared belief that the team is safe for interpersonal risk taking. It can be defined as "being able to show and employ one's self without fear of negative consequences of self-image, status or career."[126] In psychologically safe organizations, employees feel accepted and respected.

Purpose Gap – The distance between workers who find fulfillment and purpose from workers who feel disconnected and isolated from their jobs.

Resisters – An individual or group of people displaying an obstinately uncooperative attitude toward changes introduced by authoritative figures, and not threatened by disciplinary repercussions.

Second Chance Employment – Hiring individuals who have a criminal background and are ready to change their lives for the better.

Sexual Orientation – An enduring pattern of romantic, emotional, and/or physical attraction to persons of a different gender, the same gender, more than one gender, or no gender.

Stereotype Threat – The situation where people believe they are at risk to confirming stereotypes about the identity groups they belong to, and exacerbate the levels of minority stress underrepresented groups in the workplace endure.

Social Responsibility – A business principle practiced by an organization committed to balancing its revenue generating activities with its charitable investments to improve the social wellbeing of its stakeholders, including its staff, markets, and greater communities impacted by its daily operations.

Sponsor – Someone who is willing to champion the progress of a more junior colleague. A sponsor has the social capital, seniority, and clout to make a difference in the decisions other senior staff make about the progress of a more junior colleague. A sponsor recognizes your talent and believes in your abilities enough that they will risk their credibility to help a more junior colleague develop.

Straight – An adjective describing a person who is emotionally, romantically, and/or physically attracted to someone of the opposite sex. Sometimes referred to as *heterosexual.*

Talent War – Refers to an increasingly competitive landscape for recruiting and retaining talented employees. Employers eager to recruit and retain the best and brightest talent recognize their people are the key ingredient to building a successful organization.

Targeted Universalism – An approach to decision making that balances the needs of both dominant and underrepresented groups, centering approaches around those who are most vulnerable. This approach centers around equitable practices, and recognizes that when those who are most marginalized have their needs met, it benefits both underrepresented and dominant groups.

Supplier Diversity – The intentional inclusion of socially and economically disadvantaged businesses in procurement opportunities to achieve innovation, cost-reduction, and revenue growth objectives.

Transgender – An adjective that describes a person whose gender identity differs from the sex they were assigned or presumed to be at birth.

Transgender is an umbrella term that includes transgender women, transgender men, and non-binary people.

Triple Bottom Line – An accounting term evaluating a workplace's greater business value in relationship to the global marketplace as it relates to its social, environmental, and economic impact.

Unconscious Bias – Attitudes toward and stereotypes of other social groups that negatively affect our understanding, actions, and decisions in an unconscious way.

Underrepresented Groups – Describes a group of people whose members are disadvantaged and subjected to unequal treatment by the dominant group, and who may regard themselves as recipients of collective discrimination.

Workplace Ecosystem – A network of stakeholders within an organization – including employees, customers, and suppliers – working together to deliver the organization's products and/or services.

Zero Sum Game – The idea that if one-person gains something, another person loses something. When doing diversity, equity, and inclusion work, sometimes dominant groups believe that if an organization helps make underrepresented groups feel more included, they lose power, influence, and clout. The reality is that when an organization makes the DEI commitment, everyone wins.

RESOURCES

Resources

- *Belonging at Work* bonus website: www.rhodesperry.com/belong ingbook Access the site by using the password: **Belonging2018**
- Take the Implicit Association Test (IAT) here: https://implicit .harvard.edu/implicit/education.html
- Get support and guidance on cultivating workplace cultures of belonging: www.rhodesperry.com/resources

Books

- Blindspot: Hidden Biases of Good People
- Inclusion: Diversity, The New Workplace, and the Will to Change
- Everyday Bias: Identifying and Navigating Unconscious Judgments in our Daily Lives.

Videos

- Top 5 Ted Talks on Diversity & Inclusion: https://www.linkedin. com/pulse/5-top-ted-talks-inclusion-diversity-suzie-drayton
- Surprising Solutions to Workplace Diversity: https://www.you-tube.com/watch?v=mtUlRYXJ0vI&t=192s
- Diversity of Thought: https://www.youtube.com/watch?v= -4mjDiGL-V0

Book Club Discussion Questions

1. What did you already know about diversity, equity, and inclusion before you read this book? What new things did you learn?
2. What other books have you read on this topic, and how did this book differ from those that you read?
3. What feelings did this book evoke for you? Were you intrigued, overwhelmed, inspired, reflective, etc.?
4. Did you have a new perspective as a result of reading this book? Has your attitude or behavior shifted since reading this book?
5. If you had the chance to ask the author of this book one question, what would it be?

ACKNOWLEDGEMENTS

This book was 39 years in the making with a blend of lived experiences, relationships with family, friends, partners, and even those adversaries in my life who helped me understand very early what it meant to belong. Had this perfect combination of events and people not occurred, this book simply would not be in your hands.

Thank you to my Mom, Dad, and Brother for introducing me to the feeling of belonging. You all taught me the basics, and created the foundation for this book. I have deep gratitude for how you extended this feeling to so many of my LGBTQ friends and family who have struggled with receiving acceptance from their families, and to just "know" that they belong. You all are true PFLAG family, and I am so fortunate to have you in my life. I love you.

To my partner, Deanna, and my unofficial creative director, thank you for your patience as I have occupied far too many dinner time conversations, afternoon walks, bike rides, and road trips talking about this book. Your never ending abundance of support and sound judgement along with your incredible ideas influenced and shaped this book. Your genius made this final version so much stronger than my SFD. I love you.

My deepest gratitude goes to you, dear reader, for trusting me to guide you on this journey. Your curiosity and desire for greater self-awareness is what inspires me to show up every day and do my best to improve my craft. I appreciate your commitment to self-discovery, your courage to jump into unfamiliar territory, and for pushing your organization to take that journey with you. You are true workplace champions. Thank you.

To all of the brilliant folks at Publish Your Purpose Academy Press – especially Jenn T. Grace, Mark D. Gibson, and Sonia Luna – you all are truly an exceptional team. To my editor, Sarina Sandstrom, thank you for sharing my passion for the book's concept from day one! Your guidance, feedback, and judgement helped shape this book, and make it the best possible version. I appreciate your thoughts and guidance as you held my hand through this wild ride of sharing my message with the world.

For everyone who contributed to the creation of this book, I extend a deep bow of gratitude. For Senator John Perry, thank you for offering such valuable context for why this book matters in today's ever changing political and business landscape. To my first readers, thank you for strengthening the book's content. Special shout outs go to Aaron Borrelli, Rebecca Channer, Deanna Croce, Nancy Croce, Mark D. Gibson, Joseph Perry, Nancy Perry, Lisa Ruscigno, and Roey Thorpe.

To my fellow diversity, equity, and inclusion thought leaders, thank you for influencing me, and encouraging me to write this book! A huge amount of gratitude and respect specifically go to the contributors who allowed me to spend so much time interviewing, emailing, and staying in constant contact as I worked on this book. These leaders include Kylar Broadus, Jennifer Brown, Joel Brown, Ashley Brundage, Dre Domingue, and Ben Duncan.

Thank you to all of my clients past and present who believe in my firm's mission and work so hard every day to show up as the inclusive leaders you are to help your people feel a sense of belonging. Thank you for trusting me to guide you on this important journey. Together we truly are building diverse and inclusive organizations, and we are positively impacting the world socially, environmentally, and economically.

My last bit of ink for recognitions goes to my younger self for believing the future of work could include more transgender and nonbinary people. While the work is far from complete, I have a greater sense of hope when I channel my inner child who wants to live in a world where we can all be respected, valued, and celebrated for our authentic selves. Know that your older self is doing the work, and will not rest until it is complete.

NOTES

The following references were used to support the author's assertions, examples, and facts presented in this book. They include notable books, journal articles, studies, and other research. As noted in the "Start Here" section, all efforts were made to verify the accuracy of the information featured in this book as of the date of publication. You can access an online version of these references here: www.rhodesperry.com/belongingbook and use the password: **Belonging2018**.

PREFACE

1. Baumeister, R.F., & M.R. Leary (1995). The need to Belong: Desire for Interpersonal Attachments as a Fundamental Human Motivation. Psychological Bulletin, 117 (3), 497–529. Retrieved from: http://dx.doi.org/10.1037/0033-2909.117.3.497.
2. Yoshino, Kenji & Christie Smith (2013). *Uncovering Talent: A New Model of Inclusion.* Deloitte University: The Leadership Center for Inclusion. Retrieved from: https://www2.deloitte.com/content/dam/Deloitte/us/Documents/about-deloitte/us-uncovering-talent-a-new-model-of-inclusion.pdf.

INTRODUCTION

3. GLAAD (2015). *Number of Americans Who Report Knowing a Transgender Person Doubles in Seven Years, According to New GLAAD Survey.* Retrieved from: https://www.glaad.org/releases/number-americans-who-report-knowing-transgender-person-doubles-seven-years-according-new.

4. The Inclusion Lab: Tips & Takeaways for Teaching All Kids (2015). *Inclusion with a "Sparkle Effect": Q&A with Linda Mullen.* Brookes Publishing Co. Retrieved from: http://blog.brookespublishing.com/ inclusion-with-a-sparkle-effect-qa-with-linda-mullen/.

CHAPTER ONE: UNDERSTANDING DIVERSITY TERMINOLOGY

5. Dave's Killer Bread. *Second Chance Employment.* Retrieved from: http://www.daveskillerbread.com/media/second-chance -employment/.

6. Figure 1.1. Image credit: Interaction Institute for Social Change | Artist: Angus Maguire. Retrieved from: http://culturalorganizing. org/the-problem-with-that-equity-vs-equality-graphic/

7. List of Murdered Transgender People, Wikipedia. Retrieved from: https://en.wikipedia.org/wiki/ List_of_unlawfully_killed_transgender_people#2004.

8. Hass Institute for a Fair and Inclusive Society (2017). *Targeted Universalism.* Retrieved from: https://haasinstitute.berkeley.edu/ targeteduniversalism.

9. Cultural Orientations Approach. *Where You Belong: Identity Group Culture.* https://www.culturalorientations.com/Articles/ Identity-Group-Culture/67/

10. Figure 1.2. Image credit: International Women's Development Agency. What Does Intersectional Feminism Actually Mean (2017). Retrieved from: https://iwda.org.au/ what-does-intersectional-feminism-actually-mean/.

11. Yoshino, Kenji & Christie Smith (2013). *Uncovering Talent: A New Model of Inclusion.* Deloitte University: The Leadership Center for Inclusion. Retrieved from: https://www2.deloitte.com/content/ dam/Deloitte/us/Documents/about-deloitte/us-uncovering -talent-a-new-model-of-inclusion.pdf.

12. Figure 1.3. Image credit: Deloitte University: The Leadership Center for Inclusion. Retrieved from: https://www2.deloitte. com/content/dam/Deloitte/us/Documents/about-deloitte/ us-uncovering-talent-a-new-model-of-inclusion.pdf.

13. Figure 1.4. Image credit: Hall, Edward T. (1976). *Beyond Culture.* Retrieved from: https://www.amazon.com/Beyond-Culture -Edward-T-Hall/dp/0385124740.

14. Kirwan Institute for the Study of Race and Ethnicity (2015). *Understanding Implicit Bias*. Retrieved from: http://kirwaninstitute. osu.edu/research/understanding-implicit-bias/.

15. Project Implicit (2011). Retrieved from: https://implicit.harvard. edu/implicit/.

16. Ibid.

17. US Equal Employment Opportunity Commission (2018). *Sex-Based Charges (Charges filed with EEOC) FY 1997 – FY 2017.* Retrieved from: https://www.eeoc.gov/eeoc/statistics/ enforcement/sex.cfm.

18. Sue, DW (2010). *Microaggressions in Everyday Life: Race, Gender, and Sexual Orientation.* Retrieved from: https://www.amazon. com/Microaggressions-Everyday-Life-Gender-Orientation/ dp/047049140X.

19. Cambridge Dictionary Online (2013). *Discrimination, Definition.* Cambridge University. Retrieved from: https://dictionary. cambridge.org/dictionary/english/discrimination.

CHAPTER TWO: THE HUMAN NEED TO BELONG

20. Brown, Brené (2010). *The Gifts of Imperfection: Let Go of Who You Think You're Supposed to Be and Embrace Who You Are*, p.40, Simon and Schuster. Retrieved from: https://www.amazon.com/ Gifts-Imperfection-Think-Supposed-Embrace/dp/159285849X.

21. Maslow, Abraham (1943). *A Theory of Human Motivation,* Psychological Review, 50 (4), 370–96. Retrieved from: http:// dx.doi.org/10.1037/h0054346.

22. Figure 2.1. Image credit: Maslow, Abraham (1943). *A Theory of Human Motivation.* Psychological Review. Retrieved from: http:// psycnet.apa.org/record/1943-03751-001.

23. Maslow, Abraham (1954). *Motivation and Personality.* Retrieved from: http://s-f-walker.org.uk/pubsebooks/pdfs/Motivation_and_ Personality-Maslow.pdf.

24. Lieberman, Matthew and Naomi Eisenberger (2008). *The Pains and Pleasures of Social Life: A Social Cognitive Neuroscience Approach.* University of California, Los Angeles. Retrieved from: http://www. scn.ucla.edu/pdf/Pains&Pleasures%282008%29.pdf.

25. Eisenberger, Naomi, & SW Cole (2012). *Social Neuroscience and Health: Neurophysiological Mechanisms Linking Social Ties with Physical Health.* Nature Neuroscience, 15 (5), 669–74 PMID: 22504347. Retrieved from: https://www.ncbi.nlm.nih.gov/pubmed/22504347.

26. Figure 2.2. Image credit: Thoughtful Learning (2018). *What are the Social and Emotional Needs of the Brain?* Retrieved from: https://k12.thoughtfullearning.com/FAQ/what-are-social-and-emotional-needs-brain.

27. Weir, Kirsten (2012). *The Pain of Social Rejection: As Far As the Brain is Concerned, A Broken Heart May Not Be So Different From A Broken Arm.* American Psychological Association. Retrieved from: http://www.apa.org/monitor/2012/04/rejection.aspx.

28. Stanford Medicine News Center (2010). *Love Takes Up Where Pain Leaves Off, Brain Study Shows.* Retrieved from: https://med.stanford.edu/news/all-news/2010/10/love-takes-up-where-pain-leaves-off-brain-study-shows.html.

29. Hafner, Katie (2016). *Researchers Confront an Epidemic of Loneliness.* The New York Times. Retrieved from: https://www.nytimes.com/2016/09/06/health/lonliness-aging-health-effects.html.

30. The Campaign to End Loneliness. Retrieved from: https://www.campaigntoendloneliness.org/.

31. General Social Survey (2017). NORC at the University of Chicago. Retrieved from: http://gss.norc.org/

32. Framingham Study (2009). Boston Medical Center. Retrieved from: https://www.bmc.org/stroke-and-cerebrovascular-center/research/framingham-study. The 2009 study used data collected from roughly 5,000 people and their offspring from Framingham, Massachusetts since 1948 found that participants are 52% more likely to be lonely if someone they are directly connected to – such as a friend, neighbor, coworker or family member – is lonely.

33. Parker-Pope, Tara (2009). *Why Loneliness Can Be Contagious.* The New York Times. Retrieved from: https://well.blogs.nytimes.com/2009/12/01/why-loneliness-can-be-contagious/.

34. Morahan-Martain, Janet and Phyllis Schumacher (2003). *Loneliness and the Social Uses of the Internet.* Computers in Human Behavior. Retrieved from: http://www.sciencedirect.com/science/article/pii/S0747563203000402.

35. Yao, Mike Z. and Zhi-jin Zhong (2014). *Loneliness, Social Contacts, and Internet Addiction: A Cross Lagged Panel Study.* Computers in Human Behavior. Retrieved from: http://www.sciencedirect.com/science/article/pii/S0747563213003063.

36. Slater, Philip (1990). *The Pursuit of Loneliness.* Retrieved from: https://www.amazon.com/Pursuit-Loneliness-20th-Anniversary/dp/0807042013.

37. Walton, Gregory M., et al. (2011). *A Brief Social-Belonging Intervention Improves Academic and Health Outcomes of Minority Students.* Science Magazine. Retrieved from: http://science.sciencemag.org/content/331/6023/1447.

38. Ibid.

39. Ibid.

CHAPTER THREE: THE IMPORTANCE OF BELONGING AT WORK

40. Adams, Susan (2013). *Disconnected From Your Job? So Are Two Thirds Of Your Fellow Workers.* Forbes. Retrieved from: https://www.forbes.com/sites/susanadams/2013/06/12/disconnected-from-your-job-so-are-two-thirds-of-your-fellow-workers/#3ecefb37d718.

41. Yoshino, Kenji & Christie Smith (2013). *Uncovering Talent: A New Model of Inclusion.* Deloitte University: The Leadership Center for Inclusion. Retrieved from: https://www2.deloitte.com/content/dam/Deloitte/us/Documents/about-deloitte/us-uncovering-talent-a-new-model-of-inclusion.pdf.

42. Ibid.

43. Ibid.

44. Meyer, I. H. (2003). *Prejudice, Social Stress, and Mental Health in Lesbian, Gay, and Bisexual Populations: Conceptual issues and Research Evidence.* Psychological Bulletin, 129, 674–697. Retrieved from: https://www.ncbi.nlm.nih.gov/pmc/articles/PMC2072932/.

45. Goh, Joel, et al. (2015). *Exposure to Harmful Workplace Practices Could Account for Inequality in Life Spans Across Different Demographic Groups.* Retrieved from: https://www.ncbi.nlm.nih.gov/pubmed/26438754.

46. Wingfield, Adia Harvey (2015). *Being Black – but Not Too Black – in the Workplace.* The Atlantic. Retrieved from:

https://www.theatlantic.com/business/archive/2015/10/being-black-work/409990/.

47. Steele, Claude M. (1997). *A Threat in the Air: How Stereotypes Shape Intellectual Identity and Performance.* American Psychologist, 52 (6), 613–629. Retrieved from: https://kent.rl.talis.com/items/BA0A0EFA-2D0E-D5D6-1CD8-4DF7621B372F.html.

48. Certified B Corporation. *What are B Corps?* Retrieved from: http://www.bcorporation.net/what-are-b-corps.

49. Ben & Jerry's Corporate Social Responsibility Website (2018). Retrieved from: https://bjsocialresponsibility.weebly.com/index.html.

50. Cain, Susan (2013). *Quiet Power: The Power of Introverts in a World That Can't Stop Talking.* Retrieved from: https://www.amazon.com/Quiet-Power-Introverts-World-Talking/dp/0307352153.

51. Figure 3.1. Image credit: NedSpace Code of Conduct | Photo by Chelsea Lancaster. Retrieved from: http://nedspace.com/img/NedSpaceCodeofConductv1.4.pdf.

52. Balajee, Sonali S., et al. (2012). *Equity and Empowerment Lens (Racial Justice Focus).* Portland, OR: Multnomah County. Retrieved from: http://www.racialequitytools.org/resourcefiles/ee_lens_final-portland.pdf.

53. Figure 3.2. Image Credit: Balajee, Sonali S., et al. (2012). Equity and Empowerment Lens (Racial Justice Focus). Portland, OR: Multnomah County. Retrieved from: https://multco.us/file/31827/download.

CHAPTER FOUR: THE FUTURE OF WORK HAS ARRIVED

54. The Economist Intelligence Unit (2015). *Global Trends Impacting the Future of HR Management: Engaging and Integrating a Global Workforce.* SHRM Foundation. Retrieved from: https://www.shrm.org/foundation/ourwork/initiatives/preparing-for-future-hr-trends/PublishingImages/Pages/Engaging-and-Integrating-Global-Workforce/6-15%20Theme%202%20Report-FINAL.pdf.

55. United States Census Bureau (2012). *US Census Bureau Projections Show a Slower Growing, Older, More Diverse Nation a Half Century from Now.* Retrieved from: https://www.census.

gov/newsroom/releases/archives/population/cb12-243.html, and Frey, William H. (2018). *The US Will Become 'Minority White' in 2045, Census Projects: Youthful Minorities are the Engine of Future Growth.* Brookings. Retrieved from: https://www.brookings.edu/blog/the-avenue/2018/03/14/ the-us-will-become-minority-white-in-2045-census-projects/.

56. Figure 4.1. Image Credit: Agrawal, Pankaj (2016). *Introduction to the Digital World.* Retrieved from: https://www.slideshare.net/ Linkedin_Pankaj/digital-duniya-the-summer-camp-for-kids.

57. Engels, Friedrich (1958). *The Condition of the Working Class in England.* Oxford: Basil Blackwell. Retrieved from: https://play. google.com/books/reader?id=dwS-v67wuN4C&hl=en.

58. Thompson, Edward P. (1966). *The Making of the English Working Class.* New York: Vintage Books. Retrieved from: https://www.amazon.com/Making-English-Working-Class/ dp/0394703227.

59. Society for Human Resource Management (2015). *Engaging and Integrating a Global Workforce.* Retrieved from: https://www.shrm. org/hr-today/news/hr-magazine/documents/3-15%20eiu%20 theme%202%20report-final.pdf.

60. Bowcott, Owen (2014). *Uganda Anti-Gay Law Led to Tenfold Rise in Attacks on LGBTI People, Report Says.* The Guardian. Retrieved from: https://www.theguardian.com/world/2014/may/12/ uganda-anti-gay-law-rise-attacks.

61. Patricia, Anthony (2012). *Petition to Citibank Uganda Public Affairs Officer Rita Balaka: Condemn Uganda's 'Anti-Homosexuality' Law.* Change.org. Retrieved from: https://www.change.org/p/ citibank-and-barclays-condemn-uganda-s-kill-the-gays-bill.

62. Johnson, Chris, (2012). *Will Session Expire Before Uganda Acts on Anti-Gay Bill?* The Washington Blade. Retrieved from: http://www. washingtonblade.com/2012/11/30/will-ugandan-lawmakers-act- upon-anti-gay-bill-before-parliamentary-session-ends/.

63. Wingfield, Tai (2016). *Study Maps Challenges and Opportunities for Pro-Gay Companies Operating in Anti-LGBT Markets.* Center for Talent Innovation. Retrieved from: http://www.talentinnovation. org/_private/assets/OutInTheWorld_PressRelease-CTI.pdf.

64. Meyer, Erin, (2014). *The Culture Map: Breaking Through the Invisible Boundaries of Global Business.* Retrieved from: https:// www.amazon.com/Culture-Map-Breaking-Invisible-Boundaries/

dp/1610392507/ref=sr_1_1?ie=UTF8&qid=1531279136
&sr=8-1&keywords=the+culture+map+by+erin+meyer.

65. The Economist Intelligence Unit (2015). *Global Trends Impacting the Future of HR Management: Engaging and Integrating a Global Workforce*. SHRM Foundation. Retrieved from: https://www.shrm.org/foundation/ourwork/initiatives/preparing-for-future-hr-trends/PublishingImages/Pages/Engaging-and-Integrating-Global-Workforce/6-15%20Theme%202%20Report-FINAL.pdf.

66. Baker & McKenzie Global Employment Practice Group (2013). *The Global Employer: A Global Flexible Workforce – Temporary and other Contingent Workers*. Cornell University ILR School. Retrieved from: https://digitalcommons.ilr.cornell.edu/cgi/viewcontent.cgi?article=1083&context=lawfirms.

CHAPTER FIVE: MAKING THE BUSINESS CASE FOR BELONGING AT WORK

67. Riel, Jennifer (2017). Tolerance is for Cowards. Quartz at Work. Retrieved from: https://qz.com/work/1111746/tolerance-is-for-cowards/.

68. Wadors, Pat (2016). *Diversity Efforts Fall Short Unless Employees Feel that They Belong*. Harvard Business Review. Retrieved from: https://hbr.org/2016/08/diversity-efforts-fall-short-unless-employees-feel-that-they-belong

69. Figure 5.1. Image Credit: Perry, J. R. (2018). Graph source: Hurst, Aaron (2016). The Purpose Economy: How Your Desire for Impact, Personal Growth and Community Is Changing the World. Retrieved from: https://www.amazon.com/Purpose-Economy-Expanded-Updated-Community/dp/194342599X.

70. Ibid.

71. Bourke, Juliet et al. (2017). *Diversity and Inclusion: The Reality Gap*. Deloitte Global Human Capital Trends. Retrieved from: https://www2.deloitte.com/insights/us/en/focus/human-capital-trends/2017/diversity-and-inclusion-at-the-workplace.html.

72. Ibid.

73. Huppert, Maxwell (2017). *Employees Share What Gives Them a Sense of Belonging at Work*. LinkedIn Talent Blog. Retrieved from: https://business.linkedin.com/talent-solutions/blog/company-culture/2017/employees-share-what-gives-them-a-sense-of-belonging-at-work.

74. Stewart, George (2012). *Peer-Based Control in Self-Managing Teams: Linking Rational and Normative Influence with Individual and Group Performance*. Retrieved from: https://www.ncbi.nlm.nih.gov/pubmed/21895352

75. Moore, Karl (2012). *Millennials Work for Purpose, Not a Paycheck*. Retrieved from: https://www.forbes.com/sites/karlmoore/2014/10/02/millennials-work-for-purpose-not-paycheck/#4801ecbf6a51.

76. Ibid.

77. Bloomberg (2018). *What Millennials Want in Your Inclusion Program*. Retrieved from: https://www.bloomberg.com/diversity-inclusion/blog/millennials-want-inclusion-program/.

78. Peretz, Marissa (2017). *Want to Engage Millennials? Try Corporate Social Responsibility*. Forbes. Retrieved from: https://www.forbes.com/sites/marissaperetz/2017/09/27/want-to-engage-millennials-try-corporate-social-responsibility/#50bc591e6e4e

79. United States Census Bureau (2012). *Americans With Disabilities: 2010*. Retrieved from: https://www.census.gov/library/publications/2012/demo/p70-131.html

80. World Health Organization & World Bank Group (2011). *World Report on Disability*. Retrieved from: http://www.who.int/disabilities/world_report/2011/report.pdf.

81. Witeck Communications (2016). *America's LGBT 2015 Buying Power Estimated at $917 Billion*. Retrieved from, http://www.nlgja.org/outnewswire/2016/07/20/americas-lgbt-2015-buying-power-estimated-at-917-billion/.

82. Ibid.

83. Ibid.

84. Richard Fry (2016). *Millennials Overtake Baby Boomers as the Nation's Largest Generation*. Pew Research. Retrieved from: http://www.pewresearch.org/fact-tank/2016/04/25/millennials-overtake-baby-boomers/

85. United States Census Bureau. (2015). *Millennials Outnumber Baby Boomers and are Far More Diverse*. Census Bureau Reports. Retrieved from: https://www.census.gov/newsroom/press-releases/2015/cb15-113.html

86. Brookings (2014). *How Millennials Could Upend Wall Street and Corporate America*. Retrieved from: https://www.brookings.edu/wp-content/uploads/2016/06/Brookings_Winogradfinal.pdf

87. Drucker, Peter F. (2009). *Managing in a Time of Great Change*. Drucker Library. Retrieved from: https://www.

amazon.com/Managing-Great-Change-Drucker-Library/
dp/1422140792.

88. Norman, Wayne et al. (2004). *Getting to the Bottom of "Triple Bottom Line."* Business Ethics Quarterly. Retrieved from: https://www.jstor.org/stable/3857909?seq=1#page_scan_tab_contents.

89. Dun & Bradstreet (2015). *The Middle Market Power Index: The Growing Economic Clout of Diverse Middle Market Firms.* Retrieved from: http://about.americanexpress.com/news/docs/2015x/GCP-DB-Middle-Market-Wmn-Minority-Report.pdf

90. EY (2015). *How Can Greater Supplier Diversity Unclog Your Growth Pipeline?* Retrieved from: http://www.ey.com/gl/en/services/advisory/ey-five-insights-supplier-diversity.

91. Rimmer, Susan Harris, ed. (2017). *Gender-Smart Procurement: Policies for Driving Change.* Retrieved from: https://www.chathamhouse.org/sites/files/chathamhouse/publications/research/Gender-smart%20Procurement%20-%2020.12.2017.pdf.

CHAPTER SIX: UNDERSCORING THE HUMAN IMPERATIVE

92. Workforce Purpose Index (2015). Retrieved from, https://cdn.imperative.com/media/public/Purpose_Index_2015.

93. Ibid.

94. Baldoni, John (2017). *Fostering the Sense of Belonging Promotes Success.* Forbes. Retrieved from: https://www.forbes.com/sites/johnbaldoni/2017/01/22/fostering-the-sense-of-belonging-promotes-success/#59ca7d6a10f2.

95. Ibid.

96. Figure 6.1. Image Credit: Elkington, John (1997). *Cannibals with Forks: The Triple Bottom Line of 21st Century Business.* Retrieved from: https://www.amazon.com/Cannibals-Forks-Triple-Century-Business/dp/1841120847.

97. Center for Creative Leadership (2015). *Corporate Social Responsibility and Sustainable Leadership.* Retrieved from: https://www.ccl.org/wp-content/uploads/2015/04/CorporateSocialResponsibility.pdf.

98. Fridman, Adam (2016). *Purpose-Driven Entrepreneurship: The New Entrepreneurial Triple Threat: Profit, Environment, and People.* Inc. Retrieved from: https://www.inc.com/adam-fridman/the-triple-bottom-line-millennials-and-purpose-driven-entrepreneurship.html.

99. Business Dictionary (2018). *Corporate Social Responsibility.* Retrieved from: http://www.businessdictionary.com/definition/corporate -social-responsibility.html.

100. Marinova, Polina (2016). *Richard Branson to Business Leaders: Society's Problems Are Your Problems.* Fortune Magazine. Retrieved from: http://fortune.com/2016/12/07/ richard-branson-business-owners/.

101. Just Capital (2017). *JUST 100 Overall Rankings.* Retrieved from: https://justcapital.com/2017-rankings/.

102. Sinek, Simon (2009). *Start with Why.* Retrieved from: https:// startwithwhy.com/.

103. The Sustainability Imperative: New Insights on Consumer Expectations (2015). Retrieved from: https://www.nielsen.com/ content/dam/nielsenglobal/dk/docs/global-sustainability-report- oct-2015.pdf.

104. Nielsen (2015). *The Sustainability Imperative: New Insights on Consumer Expectations.* Retrieved from: https://www.nielsen.com/content/dam/ nielsenglobal/dk/docs/global-sustainability-report-oct-2015.pdf.

105. Cone Communications (2016). *Millennial Employee Engagement Study.* Retrieved from: http://www.conecomm.com/ research-blog/2016-millennial-employee-engagement-study.

106. Rhodes Perry Consulting (2018). *Supplier Diversity.* Retrieved from: http://www.rhodesperry.com/supplier-diversity/.

107. The Hackett Group Inc. (2008). *Supplier Diversity Study Results.* Retrieved from: http://www.bdrusa.org/pdf/DELETE_The_ Hackett_Group_2008_Supplier_Diversity_Study_Results_Results_ Highlights.pdf.

CHAPTER SEVEN: SERVING AS AN INCLUSIVE LEADER

108. Bourke, Juliet and Bernadette Dillon (2016). *The Six Signature Traits of Inclusive Leadership: Thriving in a Diverse New World.* Deloitte University Press. Retrieved from: https://www2.deloitte. com/insights/us/en/topics/talent/six-signature-traits-of- inclusive-leadership.html.

109. Ibid.

110. Kotter, John and Dan Cohen (2002). *The Heart of Change: Real Life Stories of How People Change Their Organizations.* Retrieved from:

https://www.amazon.com/Heart-Change-Real-Life-Stories
-Organizations/dp/1422187330.

111. Ibid.

112. Earley, P. Christopher and Soon Ang (2003). *Cultural Intelligence: Individual Interactions Across Cultures.* Stanford University Press. Retrieved from: https://www.sup.org/books/title/?id=3184.

113. Dyne, Linn Van et al. (2012). *Sub-Dimensions of the Four Factor Model of Cultural Intelligence: Expanding the Conceptualization and Measurement of Cultural Intelligence.* Social and Personality Psychology Compass. Retrieved from: http://www.linnvandyne. com/papers/Compass%202012%20Van%20Dyne%20et%20al%20 Sub-dimensions%20of%20CQ.pdf.

114. Project Implicit was founded in 1998 by three scientists – Tony Greenwald (University of Washington), Mahzarin Banaji (Harvard University), and Brian Nosek (University of Virginia). It is a non-profit organization and international collaboration between researchers who are interested in implicit social cognition – thoughts and feelings outside of conscious awareness and control. The goal of the organization is to educate the public about hidden biases and to provide a "virtual laboratory" for collecting data on the Internet. Retrieved from: https://www.projectimplicit.net.

115. Ibid.

CHAPTER EIGHT: EVERDAY ACTIONS YOU CAN TAKE, NO MATTER YOUR ROLE

116. Perry, J. R. (2017). *Beyond Lip Service: Getting Clear on How to Take Personal and Organizational Actions to Cultivate a Workplace Culture of Belonging.* Retrieved from: https://www.rhodesperry.com/blog/ belongingwebinar.

117. Kray, L. and Leigh Thompson (2005). *Gender Stereotypes and Negotiation Performance: An Examination of Theory and Research.* Research in Organizational Behavior. Retrieved from: http://www. haas.berkeley.edu/faculty/pdf/Kray_&_Thompson_ROB.pdf.

118. Navarro, Renee (2018). *What is Unconscious Bias?* University of California, San Francisco. Retrieved from: https://diversity.ucsf. edu/resources/unconscious-bias.

CHAPTER NINE: FIND YOUR NORTH STAR, SET YOUR COURSE, AND CHANGE THE WORLD

119. Wilson, Bianca D.M., et al. (2014). *Sexual & Gender Minority Youth in Los Angeles Foster Care.* The Williams Institute. Retrieved from: https://williamsinstitute.law.ucla.edu/wp-content/uploads/LAFYS_report_final-aug-2014.pdf.

120. The True Colors Fund (2018). *Our Issue.* Retrieved from: https://truecolorsfund.org/our-issue/.

121. Ibid.

122. Dobbin, Frank and Alexandra Kalve (2016). *Why Diversity Programs Fail.* Harvard Business Review. Retrieved from: https://hbr.org/2016/07/why-diversity-programs-fail.

123. Perry, J.R. & Green, E.R. (2017). *Safe & Respected: Policy, Best Practices, & Guidance for Serving Transgender, Gender Expansive, and Non-Binary Children and Youth Involved in the Child Welfare, Detention, and Juvenile Justice Systems. New York City's Administration for Children's Services.* Retrieved from: https://www1.nyc.gov/assets/acs/pdf/lgbtq/SAFEAndRespectedUpdate061417.pdf.

124. Dobbin, Frank and Alexandra Kalve (2016). *Why Diversity Programs Fail. Harvard Business Review.* Retrieved from: https://hbr.org/2016/07/why-diversity-programs-fail.

125. Sinek, Simon (2012). *Vision is a destination – a fixed point to which we focus all effort. Strategy is a route – an adaptable path to get us where we want to go [Tweet].* Retrieved from: https://twitter.com/simonsinek/status/235068415075840000?lang=en.

GLOSSARY

126. Kahn, William A. (1990). *Psychological Conditions of Personal Engagement and Disengagement a Work. Academy of Management Journal.* Retrieved from: https://en.wikipedia.org/wiki/Psychological_safety#cite_note-2.

ABOUT THE AUTHOR

R hodes Perry serves as the Founder and Chief Executive Officer of Rhodes Perry Consulting (RPC). RPC exists to support leaders, change agents, and visionaries at all levels cultivate workplace cultures of belonging. To accomplish this goal, the firm offers leadership development, strategic planning, and change management solutions designed to improve the social, environmental, and economic performance of government agencies, corporations, and nonprofits. Serving clients in nearly every part of the United States, and several international organizations, RPC continues to grow as the go-to diverse supplier offering an intersectional approach to implementing and sustaining organizational change with a demonstrated record of success, commitment, and passion.

Rhodes believes in the power of bringing authenticity into the workplace and community service. He embraces Muhammad Ali's message that "service to others is the rent you pay for your room here on Earth." He volunteers his time serving on the National Diversity Board for Studies Weekly, the Board of Directors for the Portland Area Business Association, and as a Commissioner for the Portland Human Rights Commission. He is also the host and creator of the popular podcast, *The Out Entrepreneur*, which features the power of purpose driven LGBTQ entrepreneurs.

Rhodes earned a Bachelor of Arts in Economics and Gender Studies from the University of Notre Dame, and a Master of Public Administration from New York University's Robert F. Wagner School of Public Service. He travels extensively with his bicycle around the world, and welcomes inspiration for his next great bike touring adventure.

For more information on Rhodes Perry Consulting, LLC,
please visit:
www.rhodesperry.com

For more information about *The Out Entrepreneur* podcast,
please visit:
www.outentrepreneur.com

CPSIA information can be obtained
at www.ICGtesting.com
Printed in the USA
BVHW040639160520
579795BV00009B/148/J